"In this luminous collection of stories, Annie Mattingly weaves a net of solace and insight for those of us left behind by beloveds who have died. This book blesses those moments of sweet synchronicity when the natural world becomes a portal to the place where our loved ones have gone and through which they remain ever available to us. *The After Death Chronicles* reminds us that our task is simply to be present for these encounters and allow ourselves to harvest countless gifts from beyond the veil."

—Mirabai Starr, translator of
Dark Night of the Soul: St. John of the Cross, author of
Caravan of No Despair: A Memoir of Loss and Transformation

"You don't read this book, *you savor it*: every morsel of it, every tear, every laugh, every pulse-pounding story from people so real you feel yourself akin to them. And you fall in love with Annie, snuggle right up to her and share your uttermost feelings and fears. *The After Death Chronicles* is *not* like any other afterdeath/afterlife book, nor is it really about mediums or contact with the dead. It's about real folk, Annie's people, who show you what life is and how life is lived—with or without the need to breathe."

—P. M. H. Atwater, LHD, near-death researcher
and experiencer, author of *A Manual for Developing Humans,*
Future Memory, Near-Death Experiences: The Rest of the Story, and
Dying to Know You: Proof of God in the Near-Death Experience

"*The After Death Chronicles* is must-reading for anyone who has lost a loved one. And quite frankly, that's nearly all of us. The information in this book provides solace and a great deal of hope. It's medicine for the soul."

—Christiane Northrup, MD,
New York Times best-selling author of *Goddesses Never Age*

THE AFTER DEATH CHRONICLES

THE
AFTER DEATH
CHRONICLES

*True Stories of Comfort,
Guidance, and Wisdom
from Beyond the Veil*

Annie Mattingley

HAMPTON ROADS

Cover design by Jim Warner
Cover illustration Summer Breeze, 1995 (oil on canvas), Dalton Brown,
Alice (b.1939) / Private Collection / Courtesy Fischbach Gallery, New York /
Bridgeman Images
Interior by Timm Bryson, em em design
Typeset in Adobe Garamond Pro

Hampton Roads Publishing Company, Inc.
Charlottesville, VA 22906
Distributed by Red Wheel/Weiser, LLC
www.redwheelweiser.com

Sign up for our newsletter and special offers by going to
www.redwheelweiser.com/newsletter/.

ISBN: 978-1-57174-793-8
Library of Congress Cataloging-in-Publication Data available upon request

Printed in the United States of America
M&G
10 9 8 7 6 5 4 3 2

to

my daughter Renata (Randi) Galavitz White

&

my mother Betty Ann Bender Mattingley

&

all the dead who return to bring the living solace and support

TABLE OF CONTENTS

Acknowledgments

I offer my deep gratitude to those spiritual forces and energies that led me to this work. I am grateful to my daughter Randi who helped me wind the warp on which to weave the tales that fill this book. I am immensely grateful to my entire community of friends, to my dream group, and to my family—especially to my daughter Rowena, my sister Eve, my granddaughter Chelsey, and my grandson Ollin—for all your love and support. I don't know how I could have written this book if Spencer, my beloved husband and partner for life, had not been endlessly patient with my creative peaks and valleys, morning silences, and closed door.

I am grateful to all the fabulous teachers who inspired me over the years—Sandra Delay, Vernice Solimar, Fariba Bogzaran, and Natalie Goldberg, among others. I extend my gratitude to everyone at Hampton Roads and Red Wheel/ Weiser, beginning with Greg Brandenburgh, who was eager to publish my book before he'd read half of it, to Eryn Carter and Bonni Hamilton who nudged me forward into the vast abyss of social media, and to Jane Hagaman and Ashley Benning who fixed all those pesky commas.

I give my boundless gratitude to all those who follow, most of whom generously offered me stories from their most painful times, and my apologies to those whose stories did not make it into the book. Please know that each and every one of you enriched my grasp of after-death communication and thus this book. I am grateful to those of you who read the manuscript as it progressed and to those of you who invited me to speak on my research. My heartfelt gratitude to: Edie Anderson, Barrie Andrews, Judith Myers Avis, Virginia Bartley, Linn Bayne, Therese Beck, Doug Bell, Leav Bolender, Kathleen Brennan, Pamela Buffington, Tracy Rae Clark, Camille P. Clifford, Betsy Cogburn, Bobbi Cogger, Dragica Conic, Denys Cope, Janie Corinne, Carole Crews, Cindy Rea Daniell, Jo Anne de la Fuente, Susan Dogan, Kate Drahn, Jean Ellis-Sankari, Alisa Epstein, Lucy Whyte Ferguson, Spencer Floyd, Bob Galavitz, Marie Galavitz, Rowena Galavitz, Steve Gloss, Jim Granger, Mary Griffin, Gilly Hagreen, Chuck Hammer, Kate Harris, Gordon Ian Hawley, Debbe Heiden, Gabrielle Herbertson, Stephanie Hiller, Carol Hobart, Cathy Hope, Kyoko Hummel, Chelsey Ann Hunter, Shelley Isom, Patricia Johanik, Wendy Jordan, Jenny Sue Kostecki-Shaw, Dave Krusell, Lynda Leonard, Cindy Lindsay, Jill Elizabeth MacLaren, Greg Martin, Lina Negrete Martinez, Ruben Martinez, Kathleen Matta, Eve Mattingley-Hannigan, George McKinnon, Rahmaneh Meyers, Tracy Miller, Ron Moore, June Moriyasu, Laura Olachea, Barbara Lyons Perez, Lynda Powell, Jill Pratt, Anna Racicot, Steve Racicot, Carol Rafferty, Ruth Rousseau-Clothier, Janet Schreiber, Isla Scott, Maclaren Scott, Marie Sedillo, Dr.

Lynn Sereda, Trish Sereda, Debra Solomon, Bunni Toohey, Susan Varon, Wendy Weiner, Jamie Wells, Ted Wiard, Joyce Wimer, Ariel Youst, and those who shall remain unnamed. I could not have done it without you.

PREFACE

The realm of contact with the dead lies beyond the mind's tether in a nameless, placeless land with neither topography nor maps. To explore it, we must unleash ourselves from logic and allow mystery's embrace to enfold us. We sleep on a thorny issue and in the morning reach resolution without effort. We recall a dream that brings peace to an old trouble with someone long dead. The phone rings; we know who calls. We label these glimpses by misleading names like chance or coincidence or synchronicity. We ask for a sign from a dead beloved. A bluebird appears in the heart of winter's freeze. "Impossible," we say, or "that's not big enough," having difficulty recognizing just how intertwined existence really is.

This is a book about ordinary people—plumbers and artists and accountants, bakers and beauticians, nurses, doctors, teachers, and lawyers—whose beloveds have died and who have been able to receive communication through the diaphanous veil that separates the living from the dead. It is common for us to shunt such experiences into the realm of the fantastic or the horrifying, to designate them as extraordinary and paranormal, to forget how to expect, welcome, and benefit from them. Yet here I offer demonstrations that these connections are neither horrifying nor paranormal. Nor are they rare. They are a sweet and satisfying grace from the dead who return to bring us guidance or wisdom or to reassure us they are all right.

After the deaths of my parents, a single, significant dream transformed the nature of my grieving. When I shared this, I heard other such large dreams. This planted the seed of an idea to collect them that lay dormant for years until, during the deep mourning that followed the death of my daughter, she contacted me, spoke to me, and continued to make connection morning after morning for months. When I shared these grief-altering and profound connections, I discovered they too were not unique. I heard tales of every type of after-death communication from within and around my circle of family and friends. This easy permeability of the veil between the realms of the living and the deceased was a revelation. I was inspired to seek out more such stories and to compile them into this book with the intention of opening our eyes to the illusion that these realms are separate and isolated. I interviewed my friends and family first. I hung flyers at the grocery store, the library, and on the wooden kiosks at the ends of our rural roads. Word spread. The phone rang. I received e-mails from Florida and California. I was invited to speak on my research, first at grad school grief therapy classes, then at Noetic Sciences[1] meetings, and for the bereavement and suicide survivor groups I attended after my daughter took her own life. Stories flooded in.

My interviews were informal and surprisingly intimate, considering I had often just met the other person. Though I heard stories in social settings or over the phone or through e-mail or letters, most interviews took an hour and a half to two hours and were held in coffee shop corners or living rooms or beside the irrigation acequias that run through our properties here in the northern New Mexico high desert. Wanting context, I asked: How did you get along with the deceased? What effect did this communication have on your relationship? What effect did this contact have on your life and on your relationship with death and with Spirit? Most people were eager to have their stories published, because they saw this as offering others the gift of insight into the inherent possibilities of after-death communication. A few viewed public sharing as an invasion of their privacy and conveyed their stories in confidence. I offered anonymity; some requested it for themselves, others for their dead beloveds; many didn't care, but I have changed most names and, when requested, identifying details.

I heard experiences in nearly every setting in which I met new people and the question of what I was writing arose. Nothing cut through superficial small talk like saying my book was about after-death communication. When I was asked how I got into such an area and said it was because of my daughter's visits after her death, the quality of people's attention softened and focused. This opened the floodgates to a well-kept secret: just how many of us have had at least one such contact—whether dream or voice or vision—with a deceased beloved.

People would begin, "Oh, *I've* never had an experience like that." Or "Aren't these just wishful thinking?" Then they'd end up sharing something they had never before told anyone. They'd admit, "Well, there was that one time after my mother's death . . ." and glance around as if to be sure no one could overhear, then hasten to tell me a dream or an experience with a bird, something they just couldn't shake. When my response placed the occurrence into a recognizable after-death communication pattern, faces lit up with relief, eyes brimmed with tears. Confirmation that what had happened could have been an actual connection lifted a burden of worry about their dead beloved they were not aware they carried, while it supported them to recognize the validity of their own experiences.

Even when we try to avoid it, our culture's scientific approach seeps into our language and our thought processes. We are so accustomed to hearing points of view defended or rejected based on research and studies that we may have difficulty accepting the unverifiable quality of an after-death communication and be unable to receive its benefits. Those benefits have everything to do with personal healing for the experiencer and nothing at all to do with whether the event can be verified. Claresta finds two peacock feathers in a Walmart parking lot and knows instantly that this is a communication from her deceased sister. When she feels enormously relieved, it is her knowing and her relief that are important. Attempting to assess the validity of the experience by checking to see if Walmart sells peacock feathers or whether anyone in the neighborhood keeps pet peacocks may be logical, but is it supportive to Claresta? And have we disproven the communication if we do find peacocks in the neighborhood? The true verification of an after-death contact is the value of its effect. Does it ease grief, assist with life, and relieve fears? And if it doesn't, could that mean the recipient cannot accept its validity, and might that circle us right back to the pervasive effect of the scientific approach, which can cause us to over-question even our own deepest truths?

Yet there are valid reasons we are so fearful of accepting as reality any experience that cannot be objectively verified, and it should not surprise us that people in our culture are cautious when talking about these experiences. Many experts, from psychiatrist Sigmund Freud to neurologist Oliver Sacks, pathologize contacts with the dead, labeling them as grief or bereavement hallucinations. Some of these experts are willing to admit that such grief hallucinations can be benign and even helpful. Sacks says that if they become multisensory, where touch or hearing or sight or smell are involved, or if the bereaved becomes convinced that their beloved lives on in another reality, then such "hallucinations" cross over into the world of delusion.[2] This point of view maligns anyone whose position is that consciousness does not require a physical body to exist. It maligns anyone with religious or spiritual beliefs about the existence of an afterlife. If this were the whole picture, my experience and my research indicate that it would indeed be a mad, mad world.

No one wants to be considered delusional, so the most propitious option after having contact with a deceased beloved may seem to be keeping our mouths tightly shut. If a journalist were to walk down a street with a microphone and ask the same people who have so generously shared their experiences with me if they had ever had an after-death communication, I wonder how many would reply with an immediate no. How many who do not tell me their experiences at a social gathering are simply unwilling to share with me or have buried their experiences so obscurely within their psyches they fail to recognize them as contact even to themselves?

I've been asked how I know people aren't making these stories up. Naturally, I attend carefully to people's character; I look for a sense of integrity, for how directly someone looks me in the eye, for emotion. In addition, a confirming rush of energy (what my friend Tracy Rae calls God-bumps) often ripples up my spine as I listen. I have felt this sensation for decades whenever I hear something valid, which my mind might otherwise doubt or question. I say this comes from Spirit. Others might call it intuition or say it comes from God or Buddha or Allah or Christ or the Holy Spirit, or from their guardian angels.

Once people are assured they won't be ridiculed, they are eager to share what are essentially mystical experiences that have granted them glimpses of the larger truths we yearn to know more about: that we are all interconnected and one; that death of the body is only part of the picture; that spirit, soul, consciousness, whatever we choose to call it, lives on; that our beloveds live on. The bereaved cling to these truths like a lifeline. Yet, on a level perhaps even more significant than our personal comfort, these are the truths we fumble for in our dreams, reach for in our prayers, seek out in our spiritual and religious endeavors.

Some of these experiences are permanently embedded within us. Others are more fragile; a raised eyebrow, a curled lip, too sharp of a question, can rip away what in the moment we were sure was real and of value. It is not so much the particulars that validate these contacts as the difficult to describe responses within us. Like the wings of a butterfly, these can crumble and scatter from too firm a touch. I came to see that when an experience was shared with me, only one part of my role was to listen and record accurately. At least as significant was the need to create a safe and sacred container where those fragile wings could spread unfettered.

To peruse the self-help section of a large, modern bookstore could convince us that with a few months of concentrated effort, we could accomplish any known human goal—radiant health, astonishing wealth, even complete spiritual enlightenment. I can't give you that kind of assurance. The experiences this book includes are laced with hints that support the possibility of encouraging after-death communication; my interviewees make suggestions and so do I. But the mystery of who has such experiences and why is too delicate to be controlled by a bulleted list of exercises guaranteed to bring our dead beloveds flocking. The best we can do is to encourage and be open to the possibility of contact.

The term *after-death communication*, and its acronym ADC, was coined by Bill and Judy Guggenheim during their research for *Hello from Heaven*. ADC works just as well for after-death contact or after-death connection, and I will use these terms interchangeably throughout the book. I have heard several hundred ADC experiences from more than a hundred people whose beloved dead are parents, children, pets, spouses, friends, mere acquaintances, distant and close relatives, even great-great-grandparents who died long before the person was born. Not every story is in this book, but every story has strengthened my grasp of the subject. I have interviewed people age three and a half to ninety, agnostics, Buddhists, Catholics, Eckists, Hindus, Jews, Protestants, Unitarians, the undeclared, and one atheist. Some have had their belief in an afterlife confirmed or their disbelief shattered. Without exception, everyone—including the atheist—expressed wonder and a sense of reassurance. Beyond that, responses run the gamut. A few, with the agnostic's take that we can do no more than guess about the afterlife, though they accept the veracity of their contact, don't alter their views about death at all. Some are now convinced of who will greet them when they die. One, though she has had daily contact with her dead husband for years, remains unsure she will see him when she dies, though she acknowledges feeling "less existential angst about death" than she once did. To some these contacts are so pivotal they change the course of their lives. I am one of the latter. My own innumerable and ongoing contacts with my daughter, augmented by the stories I have heard, have transformed my inclination toward an easy curiosity about the afterlife into a serene sense that not only is there absolutely nothing to fear, there also seems to be much to look forward to. The very word *afterlife* carries the implication that life is the most important state and then there is some other state. I have come to see life and the afterlife as a continuum, death not as an end but as a transition between two profoundly interconnected realms.

You will find no proof in this book, no solid, reliable evidence that after-death communication actually exists. I avoid the scientific terminology that seeks to convince us of what can only flower deep within ourselves. These narratives are anecdotal. There are plenty of people attempting to conduct scientific and empirical investigations into phenomena such as this. I am inclined to view this as a fruitless venture. ADC occurs outside the mind's ability to grasp and is not provable in the material sense that, say, the law of gravity is. Yet even as illustrious an atheist/agnostic (he vacillated) as philosopher Bertrand Russell spoke of consulting our emotions and not always relying on reason.[3]

Because the effect of an after-death contact is most often so profoundly healing, I wonder if those who are concerned about proof might be satisfied by qualitative data analysis studies in which people who claim to have had such experiences are not questioned about the veracity of their contact but about the impact of the contact on their lives. Was their grieving process changed? Were anxieties about death lessened? Did fewer of them become ill or die following the deaths of their beloveds? Perhaps studies like this would reveal to the scientifically inclined that it is results and effects that are even more significant than the experiences themselves.

Although most, if not quite all, of those whose stories this book contains would admit to at least a modicum of faith in existence beyond what reason will accept, to be engaged by this book requires neither belief nor faith nor a whole-hearted embrace of what cannot be rationally explained. It does ask that you crack a window open to the breeze of possibility that the totality of existence cannot be perceived by the mind, that there are mysteries beyond its ken, and that these mysteries are worthy of exploration. Proof and empirical evidence are concepts created to narrow experience into the confines of the human mind. There is knowing and then there is *knowing*. If I tell you I *know* my dead daughter is with me, I use the same verb I would to say I know how to drive a car or to read. In the realm of *knowing* no proof is needed, we are simply flooded with awareness from another level and from another aspect of our being.

In Isaac Bashevis Singer's short story "Inventions," a Communist theoretician encounters the ghost of a dead acquaintance and attempts to call it a hallucination. He can neither dismiss the questions this raises nor accept this is a ghost, for to do so would force him to change his worldview.[4] This man's world is defined by the Communist ideology, which excludes the religious or the spiritual. We often define existence according to an organization or a system of beliefs that comes from our culture or our field of study or our families, rather than from actual experience. If I had never been aware of contact with a dead beloved, the very thought might violate the tenets of my belief system. But can a belief or a worldview be malleable and open to change? Can hearing the stories of others' experiences open us to our own?

If you are starting this book with a few questions, I hope you will finish it with more, since I propose that questions may be of more value than answers. When we have an answer, we can stop our inquiry, feel complete and satisfied, but an unanswered question invites our continued attention. I hope, long after you lay this book aside, you continue to ponder the imponderables, which implies, in Webster's words, *prolonged, inconclusive thinking about a subject incapable of being weighed or evaluated with exactness,* like the questions: Why are we here? Why do we die? What is death? Does some part of us survive beyond it? If so, what is that part? What about free will? Are we destined to die when we do and will we live again? Exploring after-death communication is like diving into the heart of a thousand-petaled lotus. The more questions I ask, the more arise; the more I learn, the less I know. For me, it is a continual process of discovery. I wish the same for you.

INTRODUCTION

*Negative Capability, that is, when a man is capable of
being in uncertainties, mysteries, doubts, without any
irritable reaching after fact and reason.*
    —**John Keats, Letter to George and Thomas Keats**

I could have distilled this book's essence into the single sentence: The dead return to let us know they are okay. The
two words, "I'm okay," are the ones most often quoted to
me from the dead. When the dead use other words, or none
at all, their presence alone conveys the same sense and offers
powerful healing. The bereaved frequently suffer the twin
tortures of guilt and blame. Whether the death is from illness, accident, old age, or sudden violence like suicide or
murder, our grief-flooded thoughts may replay every nuance
of every choice we made over the last days or hours or minutes of our beloveds' lives like destructive mantras, beating
up on ourselves as if doing so could disentangle us from
death's grip. We ask ourselves, "Why didn't he . . . she . . .
they . . . I . . . ?" You fill in the blank. The dead visit us to

stop this terrible process. They come to say, I'm not in my body, yet I exist and I am not suffering. They come to reassure us that however we may wish it otherwise, this is how it is and it is okay. Remember, they may say, we decided together to wait to go to the ER. I participated in that decision with you. A significant part of their message may be, You are not to blame for my death.

I spent my first half-century on the East and West Coasts of the United States, where light pollution, air pollution, and humidity mask the night sky. It wasn't until I moved to the high desert that I experienced the wonder of being able to step out my back door under the magnificent canopy of a visible Milky Way. It had always been there, of course; I just hadn't been able to see it. The other planes of existence are like that, masked by the fact that we look for them with our minds and our physical eyes.

We have other, more ineffable, ways of seeing. At my father's deathbed, how did I "see" his essence leave his body? To answer this directly requires a rationality that might suppress what I experienced. Our human mind and our physical eyes have only so much ability to plumb the deep enigmas. We use these tools to evaluate the world around us, to decide if we are really driving toward a lake not on our map or a mirage. It's not necessarily inappropriate that concern over being gullible can make us doubt the most mystical of experiences. We've heard about those séances where Grandpa had the task of sitting in the room below and tapping on the ceiling with a broomstick at the appropriate moments. The same love that can open the door to invisible worlds can also make us turn a blind eye to the wiles of our own imaginations. The

mystical path is a narrow cliff to be traversed with an oxymo-
ronic synergy of boldness and caution. How we discern what
is real, what is charade, is a task beyond teachers or books.
We must digest the subtle signs and determine their validity
within our deepest, least easily accessed parts.

Our worlds interpenetrate. They exist simultaneously.
Our beloved dead are among us as clearly as the Milky Way
is above us. Initially I thought it was the pollution of our
fears and doubts that could cloud our ability to receive contact. My daughter told me she visited people who did not
know she was there. I watch one friend long for a visitation
from her daughter she either doesn't receive or isn't aware
of. I have come to view as hubris any claim to know why
this is so. Each of us receives, or doesn't, according to factors
larger than our limited human minds can decipher. If we do
become aware of a visitation, its power is layered. The gilded
outer shell is the blessing of connection with our beloveds.
Within this shell is the eloquently simple seed of awareness
of life's continuity.

The more transcendent an experience is, the more difficult it is to convey its full depth and richness, so language
is at issue here. Words are like sieves, designed to contain
dense matter; the fine grains of the transcendent may sift
through, leaving behind only faint traces of their essence.
Even the words "the living and the dead" are inadequate. If
it weren't so cumbersome, I'd use "those of us with physical
bodies and those of us without physical bodies," for if beings
can speak, make themselves visible, shine as a light, cause
rivers of energy to move though our bodies, unplug phones,

demonstrate their love, how well does "dead" really describe them? They lack physical bodies, that's all. One interviewee told me the Aramaic word for *dead* translates to "not here but elsewhere," adding, "not *physically* here." Another pointed out that even calling where the dead are "the other side" is problematic, for to do so denies their presence here among us. Words cannot describe this kind of interpenetration.

꿍

Within our Western literary canon, there are many references to contact with the dead. Shakespeare's *Hamlet* centers on an after-death communication from Hamlet's father. Charles Dickens' *A Christmas Carol* is all about Marley's visitation to Scrooge. In Ibsen's *The Lady from the Sea* it is a deceased lover who woos the lady. In the ancient worlds, or in cultures that have retained their older traditions, such contact is expected and sought after. Mexicans celebrate *El Dia de los Muertos*, Day of the Dead. On November 1, *las almas chicas*, the dead children, are invited to return, and on November 2, *las almas grandes*, the adults, are invited. They are coaxed here with favorite food and drink on fanciful and exquisite home altars and after a visit are urged to return to the land of the dead. In Oaxaca, where *Muertos* rivals Christmas in importance as a holiday, I have seen *las ancianas*, the older women, sit either by these altars or in the graveyards in communion with their dead beloveds round the clock. All over the globe similar days are celebrated at the same time of year, like the Celtic Samhain on October 31 and the Hopi and Zuni Ancestors' Day on November 2.

As many who have contact with the dead, including myself, experience, the veil between the living and the dead thins at this time of year. Our culture is aware of this, too, but the knowledge has mutated into sheet-draped ghosts and masked ghouls. How we celebrate Halloween negates the possibility of receiving love and support from the dead. Mainstream modern culture denies after-death communication as anything but an aberration. This denial is a mass deprivation of our human right and capacity to have continued contact with our deceased beloveds, who long to show their love, to support us, to let us know they are doing okay.

The traditions of every indigenous group I have explored include seeking wisdom and guidance from the dead. I have taken part in rituals in traditional Fijian villages where the *Darne Vuthu's*, or shaman's, role is to seek out this wisdom. The Hopi fashion special cylindrical "bucket" masks to assist in calling back the dead. Various peoples call in the ancestral spirits for help with everything from making tools to moving into a new home. To the African Shona people, those dead who return to teach and support us are matured and purified.[1] I have experienced this maturing with my daughter, and I have heard of it from others. Crossing the veil may make us invisible (not always!), but it also frequently transforms us. An innate generosity and wisdom often arise. When we are no longer restricted to our finite physical bodies, we seem more able to see the full picture of each situation, as if the act of dying strips us of blinders and sets our priorities straight. A woman apologizes to her deceased husband for certain regrets in how she had related to him.

He responds, as if with a shrug, It's okay, nothing more than a row of pins, so let that go. What may have mattered to him in life, in death has lost its significance; it is only their love that concerns him now.

Years ago when my beloved dog Geefer was struck and killed by a car, I was told it would upset me too much to see his body, but I chose to anyway. I was stunned by the absolute clarity of his absence. This was only the slack, cold body of some beautiful black dog who looked a lot like my Geefer. At my father's viewing I stayed away from the open coffin. At the end of his funeral, when I gathered all my scattered parts to approach him, I stifled a rueful laugh. One eyebrow had been cocked into an unfamiliar expression. Familiar wrinkles had been smoothed. His complexion had been "enhanced" with foundation and rouge and powder. Had my father ever for one second considered that someone might rouge his cheeks, he would have stipulated in his will: Absolutely No Makeup. As I gazed at him, I wondered why I had worried so about seeing his body, because he was not in it. Later I wondered what the point was of viewing this collection of cells that I had once identified as my father. Yet I had needed to look at the empty bodies of both my dog and my father to clarify the separateness of their two aspects. It seems that grief and loss make us forget about this, or maybe it's simply plain old habit. I was used to my dog and my father being synonymous with their bodies. It is easy to mistake the external for the internal, the description of a dream for its wonder, our bodies for our enigmatic essence, when it is the essence that is our true self. It is this true and eternal self that makes contact through the veil, and it is this eternal self that we recognize when contact is made.

The experiences that follow are as varied as the people who have shared them with me—some are visual, some auditory, some visceral, some subtle, some as life-affecting as near-death experiences. They range through dreams, disembodied voices, visions, electrical and physical manifestations, messages received through nature. They can be the rare frightening contact or a profoundly satisfying grace that precedes or follows a death or occurs at the moment of death. They can happen in a flash or transport us into an extended altered state that lasts all day. Visitations can come once or continue repeatedly for years. They can contain nothing but that relieving "I'm okay" or grant anything from a glimpse to a rich understanding of what we have come together to accomplish in our lives together.

These experiences have defied my early efforts at neat categorization—dreams here, visions there, visitations through nature given their own chapter. What I found was that if a man has a dream *and* a vision *and* a nature experience, to separate these was to lose the rich story of the man himself. The stories are woven together like a tapestry; though chapter 2 focuses on dreams, there are also dreams threaded into almost every other chapter. This method suits the subject matter more effectively anyway. After-death connection is neither rational nor orderly. We don't have labeled pockets in our psyches in which to file such moments.

Like a sonnet or a symphony, an ADC is more than the sum of its parts. These moments speak to us in the language of Spirit or God or the universe. They are not intended to be fully understood but rather to be savored and allowed to delight. More than anything else they resemble poetry, which, as Paul Valéry says, is defined by being indefinable.[2] They imprint themselves indelibly on our memories as being different from other moments in time. I ask as you read that you hold these stories as tenderly as you would a newborn. I ask that you receive them as they were experienced, as precious offerings from someone dearly loved, that you not allow the two-dimensional black and white of the page to diminish them. There is something in them that is unfathomable, even to the one experiencing them. Under too much dissection they may disintegrate.

Chapter One

RANDI, IS THAT YOU?

They just knew something that is,
from time to time, forgotten except by the wind.
How close the dead are. One song away from the living.
—**Louise Erdrich,** The Master Butchers Singing Club

Goose bumps ripple up my left side. Opening an eye, I cringe at how dawn barely brushes the window with faint light before burrowing back into sleep's amnesiac blanket. I strain to ignore the second rush, too. Because each moment I do not think of my daughter's death, it ceases to be true, every morning she dies anew, so I push to sleep past first remembering. When this river of energy courses through my entire body a third time, I sit up, confused, a little scared, and also, I suppose now, more than a little curious. "Randi, is that you?" I ask aloud, having no conscious awareness of why I would even think of such a bizarre question. "If it's you, give me a sign, move something, do something, so I know." For a moment the morning holds its breath.

Then I hear my daughter's dear and familiar voice say, Your body knows. There is a long beat while I mentally check out my body. She is quite right. My body—not my mind, which is still in a state of shock—*does* know. It knows this is my daughter's voice. It knows she is there with me. And most relieving of all, my body knows that she is all right. It is as though a wide doorway has been opened into an immense cathedral of possibility, allowing me to continue on. It is too small to say that I know my daughter is all right, because that knowledge bridges a chasm between my abject misery over her suicide and the cusp of new hope.

The cusps of things, the ineffability of consciousness, of conception and birth and of death and the process of dying, the mystical realms, have long been the heart center of my life. I attend to my dreams. I have sat with the dying. I am captivated by the enigma of death. I have studied and meditated on and prayed and done shamanic journeying over, avidly read about, and endlessly discussed the great mysteries all my life. How it is that I never before attended to the possibility of direct contact with our dead beloveds now seems to me a mystery in itself. It is as though the whole subject had been held in abeyance until the fruit of my life had ripened into this moment.

Soon the idea that the dead can speak became my daily reality. In the early morning hours of almost every day for many months, my formerly troubled, depressed, and pain-wracked daughter came to talk with me. I put a special "Randi Messages" notebook on my nightstand. Her visitations always began with that tingling, goose-bumpy rush, and that rush always came up my left side. Then we held internal conversations. That first morning was to be the only time I have ever heard her voice aloud outside my own head. She controlled the parameters of our exchanges. I could not invoke her presence, and I have never been able to see her. There were subjects she would not touch, like the last sixteen months of her life or her death or where on earth she had put her original will.

The next few pages have kept me awake nights pondering how best to handle writing about her death. Every author from Shakespeare to the romance novelist knows that one sure way to evoke tears and tug on heartstrings is to insert the death of a child, and any son or daughter, regardless of age, is still a child to a parent. This is the death that should never be, we are told, the one out of the natural order of life. Yet the moment my daughter died, I was initiated into a large clan of those whose children are dead. This book is a synthesis of research and personal experience that covers both objective and subjective realities, and to simply graze past my daughter's death, as I have so far, could give the false impression that our after-death connection stripped away all suffering. I fear this narrative might then collapse into the way we in our culture tend to bypass grief with pat phrases like, "I'm sorry for your loss," spoken without emotion, while not looking someone in the eye.

I fall back here, Dear Reader, on this old-fashioned method of addressing you, because sharing such an intimate aspect of my life requires that I consider you dear. I look you in the eye as I give you now a hint of what this most horrific circumstance was like for me. Then I will go on to the after-death communications I have experienced and been told about and their astonishing ability to transform and to heal.

&

I make no attempt to imagine when my daughter's dying began for her, in the depths of her psyche, but for me it began on a Sunday, the day after her forty-sixth birthday. It was May and still chilly in Colorado. She was still in bed. She was often still in bed then, or already in bed. Her bed was full of pillows and the pillows were full of dog and cat hair. Probably Angel, her blond dog, and maybe Shiloh, her blond cat, were on the bed with her. I don't remember. What I do remember is the tone of her voice, thin as a thread stretched taut and more full of suffering than any voice I have ever heard. I remember the animal hairs on her black cotton T-shirt, the way her back curved in on her body as she spoke.

"After Chelsey is out of college," she began, staring at her knees, "or maybe after she's married, I don't know. And after the animals die, I guess, all of them, after they all die," she said, "I won't be here."

"What do you mean, you won't be here?"

"You know," she shrugged. I didn't. Her voice was flat, as though she were telling me about going to the grocery store. "I won't be here." She said more, like that God surely wouldn't let her feel so much pain in heaven. More. Once it finally penetrated that she was circling around that she would be dead, and by her own hand, my vision went fuzzy, my breath ragged. Her words sliced me open. I longed to cuddle her on my lap, and then to take charge. "You can't do this—not to yourself, not to me, not to Chelsey. I will not allow it." Yet as I looked at her stricken face and body, I felt I had no right, that to say such words would be to sentence her to an infinite amount of suffering. What did I know of how it was to live for twenty-five years with chronic pain from being kicked in the jaw by her horse? What did I know of her inner demons? When I touched her, her body was brittle and resistant. When I spoke, she resisted my words of love in the same way. I made fervent, silent vows about supporting her through and beyond this.

The next sixteen months were our family's private hell as she spiraled down and away from us. She made a mild suicide attempt. She was demoted from her position as head of the doctors in the women's clinic where she worked as an ob-gyn. She went through the motions of psychotherapy and psychiatry, yet she did not seem to benefit. She made a second, more serious suicide attempt. Eventually her short medical leave became a long one, and finally her job contract was not renewed. She went on permanent disability. Despite the efforts of many, she stored up her prescribed pain medication and took her own life. Her daughter Chelsey had only just started her first semester in college. Angel the dog and Shiloh the cat were still very much alive, and Speedy the turtle was, too. For me, those months were a reverse gestation, ending in my desperate call for a police well-check, a reverse labor where her life, instead of beginning with a cry, ended in what I assumed (incorrectly!) would be the eternal silence of her death.

At first the refrigerator was a baffling cave, the stove a confusion of knobs. Others cooked. I ate what was put before me. Who knows when I changed my underwear or brushed my teeth, though I anchored myself in Spirit. Every day without fail I did my mantra practice; in this way I did not become totally unmoored. And rather to my surprise, I got through the days and somehow a few weeks passed. It was then that her visitations began.

These offered more succor than I could ever have hoped for. For now, I'll give you just one example. She was giving me guidance as I explored a dream, clarifying a significant understanding. As happened sometimes if a visitation went beyond fifteen minutes or so, I began to tire. My mind wandered back to one or another of the difficult moments toward the end of her life. It felt as if she leaned forward and laid her hand tenderly on my thigh. Mom, she murmured, do you think you could let go of that stuff now? Had anyone else, no matter how well-meaning—husband, friend, therapist—asked this of me back then, I would have been staunchly defensive—arguing, *Are you crazy? I don't know how to let go of this.* Instead, the memory was totally erased as if my mind had been magically wiped clean, the first infinitesimal step in releasing my suffering over her dying and her death. Her wisdom and guidance, not of this plane, carry a different weight than what comes from those of us in the physical. The strength of our months of nearly daily communication was so healing and so empowering I longed to do something to let the world know just how close our beloved dead can be. When the idea came to me to write this book, Randi endorsed it passionately.

Since then, through my interviews, I have come to understand how much the dead want the living to be aware of their presence among us, just as we all yearn to be recognized and acknowledged by those we know and love.

෮ඁ

My communications with my daughter, which are related in more depth in chapters 3 and 8, as well as here and there throughout the book, were primarily verbal and felt in the body, but—as you are about to find out—visitations come in as many guises as there are people to die and return to visit us. I will start by introducing you to a patchwork quilt of ADC expressions from their vast and colorful array. One common way for the dead to make contact is through some aspect of the natural world, especially with birds and butterflies. I have often migrated south to the Mexican colonial city of Oaxaca for the winter. My community there includes my Spanish teacher, Flor. When I shared what I was writing, she said, "*Tengo un cuento para ti.* I have a story for you. My mother has been visiting me as a white butterfly ever since her death." Flor's sister scoffed derisively when told of these visitations, until a white butterfly began coming to her so often, and so uniquely, that now she too fully accepts this as an after-death communication.

A decade of these butterfly visitations has passed. Flor's twenty-year-old niece Sandra is visiting from the States. "*Tu abuelita*, your grandma, still comes to me as a white butterfly," Flor tells her.

"*Tía*, that's crazy. I don't believe that stuff."

"You'll see," Flor answers. Later, as they stroll through Oaxaca's Parque Llano, Flor points out a white butterfly off to the side. "There's your grandma," she says, stopping on the path.

"It is not!"

"It is."

"Okay," Sandra thrusts her arm and pointed finger like a sword at the butterfly. "If you are my grandma, you come right over here!" she demands, signaling with her finger two inches in front of her chest. As if yanked by a leash, the white butterfly zooms to her chest and Sandra's view of contact with the dead instantly alters. She bursts into tears, feeling certain that the essence—not the body, of course, but some equally recognizable aspect of her beloved grandmother—is there with her. This has swept away the skeptic in her. Flor's assistance has helped Sandra to step outside her rational mind long enough to experience with another part of herself someone she has known and deeply loved.

By so freely sharing her ADC experience, without concern for ridicule or skepticism, Flor (with the help of her mother and the butterfly) has opened two relatives to visitations from their mother and their grandmother. Now the white butterfly comes often to Sandra back home in Texas. I say "the" butterfly, fully aware that there are many butterflies, but also aware that to cultures that honor and respect the energies of nature's creatures, one eagle or one butterfly represents all eagles, all butterflies.

❧

Once again, simply by mentioning this book, though this time in English, I heard a story. My multitalented hairdresser Lauren, who is also an accomplished fine art photographer and documentary filmmaker, told me the following as she cut my hair. She had been at her computer, behind her the larger-than-life photo of her dad she had taken toward the end of his life, his oxygen cannula prominently in view, when she noticed two disparate odors. The first was clearly liverwurst. The second, equally as definitive, was that of A&D Ointment. Then came the pivotal moment—the one that initiates us into another realm. She swiveled her chair around, faced the photo, asked, "Dad?" and received an answer. Inside her head, she and her deceased father engaged in as lengthy and as satisfying a conversation as though he were physically present.

"Why liverwurst?" I asked. A favorite food of his, Lauren told me, and one he had been urged to eat to keep his blood pressure up. "And A&D Ointment?" It was what the family had used on his diapered bottom as he lay dying at home. What else could have been more specifically and uniquely connected to her father, nearly instantly recognizable, even so out of context and long after his death?

Because I don't have a particularly well-developed sense of smell, I may never have an olfactory visitation, and I have not been told of many, but for some, smell is what opens the door into the other worlds. Two women mentioned the scent of a man's pipe smoke. One experienced this in impossible places like her college dorm room, with the comforting sense that her deceased grandfather was checking to see how she was doing. The second woman's family and friends reported smelling her dead husband's pipe smoke so many times it made her jealous. Why wasn't he visiting her?

I have heard similar complaints from others lost in the abyss of grief. Sometimes the closest people are not the ones to receive contact. I suspect this is because, as much as they yearn for it, they might be too disturbed if a visitation did happen. This young widow had been bursting into tears in the produce aisle of the grocery store at the sight of broccoli—her husband's favorite vegetable. Can you imagine the overwhelming emotions the scent of his pipe smoke at home might have stirred up within her? Perhaps the dead avoid stirring up such strong emotions within themselves as well.

❧

Few of us are born seers or psychics, but the ability to experience and to recognize a visitation appears to be a skill we can develop. The first surprising one may awaken our inner vision and lead us to the second. It is as though once we have slashed a path through the jungle of the mind, we can more easily follow that path later. Many people shared numerous experiences with me. This may not be because they have been endowed with some special skill, but because, through their own experience, they have learned how to continue receiving in this way.

Susan is one example. At the time that her husband Jesse died of unexpected issues with a blood disorder, I had known them for all but the first few of their forty-five-year marriage. A former kindergarten teacher turned psychotherapist, Susan reminded me, as she began to share her experiences, that she was not prone to the mystical, and she had neither looked for nor expected a visitation from Jesse. She told me how she cherished the memory of the two of them listening to classical music together. The emotional pull of music was so intense that after his death she had avoided it completely, until friends, to distract her, whisked her off to a student recital, where an unassuming teenage boy ambled up to the piano. To Susan's surprise, he gave a thrilling performance. In the presence of such exquisite sound, she relaxed, and her relaxed state allowed her to "half-see, half-sense" Jesse. Up until that moment, she says now, "My myopic grief kept the channel closed."

Thus began an adventure that has continued for years. She can physically feel his body and his touch. He comforts her, holds her, rocks her. He warns her to slow down when she doesn't notice that the traffic has stopped up ahead. When she couldn't find an essential item for their swimming pool, she asked, "Jesse, where did you put it?" He told her which outbuilding to enter, which direction to turn once she did, and precisely which shelf to look on; there the part was. At the close of her first yoga class, as she lay on her back relaxing in Savasana pose, he plopped himself facedown on top of her. She was as astonished as she was tickled. When I told her that Savasana pose is also called Corpse pose, we were both convinced he was aware of this pun. Susan has always considered his sense of humor one of the best aspects of their relationship, since she tends to take life quite seriously; it seems he's still helping her with this.

Susan describes his presence as surprisingly undeniable, not obscure at all, as she might have imagined, had she ever imagined such a contact were possible. She says attuning herself to Jesse's presence has transformed her previous skepticism. Now, though this would never have been possible prior to Jesse's contact, she is able to converse with both of her deceased parents. Of Jesse, she says, "He is never more than a breath away." His presence is so definitive to one of their young granddaughters that she holds doors open an extra moment so her granddad can come through, too.

Another deceased man's grandson warns his father to take care when pulling the car away from the shoulder of the road onto the highway because, "Grandpa's right in front of the car." A moment later he adds, "It's okay now, he's gone to see Grandma." Grandma, when asked if she's had contact with her husband, says, "Well, yes, he did visit me." This couple had had what could generously be called an acrimonious relationship, full of verbal jabs and jibes; basically, they fought constantly. On this morning, Grandma, who is not well, is tired out from making the bed. She sits resting on a chair, when her husband appears before her.

"What are you doing here?" she demands.

"Oh, I thought I'd just stop by for a little sex."

"Hey, you're the one who left me, so I guess you're out of luck," she snaps. He fades away without another word.

இ

Another way the dead reveal themselves is through physical objects. They are particularly adept with lights, electrical equipment, and electronics, and they really can make things go bump in the night, though their actions seem more like a child's efforts to get our attention than the frightening way these are often portrayed. This ADC type may vary from amusing to downright annoying; it is startling to see how instantly people can recognize who is causing these incidents to occur.

Lillian was widowed by her husband's sudden accidental death. He had been a scientist who liked to work long after she had retired for the night. Much later she would be awakened by the sounds of him undressing before he slipped his chilled body in beside hers, where she would warm him with her own bed-warmed body. For several months after his death, though he never joined her in the bed, she heard the familiar sound of him unbuckling his belt. This was a comfort and seemed natural to her, she told me. Natural seems to me the perfect word for an ADC—just as it ought to be.

This was not the only way Lillian's husband contacted her. Several times in the middle of the night, she was awakened by her doorbell ringing, "loud and clear." She knew at once this was his doing, and it even happened when she was staying at her daughter's home. Lillian told me that in about the thirtieth year of their forty-six-year marriage, they had put some special attention on enlivening their romantic life. One day he had left the house without her knowing, and on his return, instead of letting himself in, he rang the doorbell, holding a bouquet of flowers for her behind his back. The ringing doorbell reminds her of that old romantic gesture. He no longer enters the bedroom to undress or rings the doorbell either, yet she says there are still times when she can sense his presence. In addition, because now she knows how to, she is able to sense her deceased mother-in-law's presence.

⤫

Kim, a Canadian family therapist and professor emerita I interviewed in The Italian Coffee Company in Oaxaca, shared with me how for six months following her mother's death the security alarm in Kim's home kept going off for no reason. From the very first time, Kim thought her mother was making this happen. Finding nothing wrong, the alarm company came up with vague justifications like that "a big truck must have gone by." The malfunctions frequently happened when Kim and her husband were in Toronto where her mother had lived. One occurred when they were there to sign the papers for the sale of her mother's home. Kim's husband would not accept that this was his mother-in-law making contact. When the alarm issues ceased, he said, "See, 'they' finally fixed it," even though "they" had never admitted to finding anything wrong with the system. This problem with the alarm was "annoying, exasperating, sometimes quite inconvenient," yet Kim told me she found it "reassuring to sense that my mother was nearby and keeping watch." Again we see a very personal clue. An alarm system is something to protect us, just as mothers do. When Lillian's husband rang the doorbell, it hinted at romance, even playfulness.

⤫

Picture the following scene. On this evening the power has gone out. Isabel sits alone on her living room couch, before her the two identical candles she has lit to dispel the darkness. Undistracted by all those activities that normally fill our evenings, she is thinking of her deceased father: *If he were to visit me, I wonder how he would let me know he's here?* At this query, as if put out by a candle-snuffer, one—only one—of the candles goes dark. Her question is answered: her father is there with her, and she knows it.

This situation illustrates something about how we receive after-death contact. Isabel is alone. She is quiet and undistracted. She asks a simple question of her dead father, without too much longing in it. She awaits the answer. It's like nourishing and watering a flower, giving it just the right amount of sun. A calm and listening attentiveness can create an opening for our beloveds to make connection, allowing their presence to bloom within us.

∽

The most frequent way our beloved dead make connection with us is through dreaming, which is the altered state of consciousness most readily accepted by the most number of people. ADC dreams are not simply *about* the dead or *with* the dead. They are particularly vivid, especially easy to recall, and often they come bearing gifts. In the following two dreams, these gifts contain important guidance.

My interview with Lenore took place in The Taos Inn, known locally as "the living room of Taos" for its pleasant atmosphere of comfortable couches and a corner kiva fireplace. Lenore was comfortable to be with, too, as well as artistically talented and happily married. She said she had been single a few years earlier as she traveled back and forth across the country to help care for her dying mother. Her mother had never been a religious or spiritual woman, but in her final months she asked to see a minister and began to speak of God and the afterlife and of meeting Lenore after she crossed over. During this time, the two women grew closer. "We healed our relationship," was how Lenore put it. Perhaps half in jest, she had asked her mother to, "Send me a man, Mom." Soon Lenore did begin to see a new man, though she wasn't sure he was "the" one.

Lenore's ADC experience begins with an instance of synchronicity, a contact that may be difficult to recognize and defend to a skeptic. Nine months after her mother's death, hospice gave a Christmas party for the families of those who had died during that year. Lenore flew back to attend with her family and was instructed to select a name tag under her mother's name. Flipping through the box, she couldn't locate it under the letter M, so she went right to W with the quirky idea that maybe the name tag had been misfiled by a dyslexic person. What she found was not her mother's name but the very uncommon last name of her new gentleman friend. With that knowing that an ADC so often brings, she instantly took this to be a sign of her mother's approval.

Yet Lenore did not fully commit to this relationship until she had received dream guidance from her mother. In a dream her mom called her into Lenore's former partner's bedroom. When Lenore sat on the bed with him to her left, her mom to his left, her mom immediately stood up, declaring, "No! Verne is in the way!" and moved to sit between them. Again the meaning was obvious to Lenore: she needed to resolve some attachment to this prior relationship in order to commit to her current one. With this dream pointing the way, she worked through her issue, clarified the depth of her love for this man, and married him.

Later Lenore had another dream in which she said, "Oh, Mom, I miss you." Her mother replied, "Don't miss me, love me," in that very no-nonsense manner the dead can have. They don't go in for idle small talk, and they don't avoid what they view as important. The distinction her mother makes has relevance to after-death communication in general, because of how too much longing (or missing) or very intense grief can block contact.

Though in a totally different context, Kerry's dream gives guidance from her deceased mother as well. Kerry had traveled to support the birth of her daughter Sally's first child at the end of a challenging pregnancy. After Sally had a few contractions, she felt ready to go to the hospital, but her family, which included a physician, all felt this was premature, so everyone went to bed. In the morning, Kerry awakened from a dream in which her deceased mother told her, Don't doubt your daughter. You need to tell the doctor. Just get going, which they did. The birth was normal, but what was interesting is that the doctor said the placenta was "old," and they ought to have come to the hospital the night before.

እን

My friend Anne Kious, a Tibetan Buddhist and retired accountant, was immediately fascinated by the subject of this book. During the process of my research and writing, she contracted melanoma. It metastasized and, after various treatments, she was at home, preparing to die. I was only one of numerous neighbors who took turns bringing her food. On this day she invited me to join her for lunch. It was the last time she would be strong enough for me to maneuver her into the wheelchair and to the table. As we ate, she inquired about my book. It was so like Anne to be nearing death and yet remember how important this project was to me. We ended up arranging that she would make contact with me after her death. Such a plan was a first for me.

"How will I know it's you?" I asked. By way of reply, she told me about the time a bird had flown down her chimney and gotten stuck inside her woodstove. When she pulled it out, it was limp and so ash-covered she couldn't tell the color of its feathers. She tenderly cleared its beak and face so it could breathe, wiped its wings clean, carried it outside. "It was the most stunning swallow with the most gorgeous colors," she told me. "I opened my hands, and it flew off into the sky, back into life." Her face shone with how joyful that release had been for her. Anne said it was . . . well, actually I promptly forgot what kind of bird she had called it. Had she said violet? A swallow, that much I knew. I kept meaning to look it up. I kept forgetting, probably because to look it up meant focusing on her death. Anne died late the next Tuesday night, but because I was gone all the next day, I did not hear of her death until Wednesday night.

Early the following morning, I went into my yard to work off some of my sorrow. This was the first time since her death that I'd been outside except to go to and from my car. Anne was very present in my mind. Our arrangement was not, but when a bird began circling me, I flashed on our plan. This bird circled like swallows do, but it didn't look like any swallow I recognized. A pair of western bluebirds flew into our nest box. This was startling, since the nestlings had fledged and flown off a while back, so I put down my clippers to watch them. Now the first bird was circling both me and the nest box, flashing white on every turn. I thought, *does any swallow have this much white?* Once the bluebirds flew off, this bird made one more graceful arc around me before perching on the front of the nest box in perfect profile, where it remained, while I crept closer and studied its white head and belly, its gorgeous, iridescent green back, its grayish wings. *Don't all swallows have long, forked tails?* I couldn't see any tail at all, nor could I see any violet. *This bird cannot be Anne,* I thought. *It isn't a swallow, and it isn't violet.* Suddenly my feet and ankles were burning and stinging. To my chagrin I discovered I was standing in the center of a small ant's nest. "All right, all right, I'll go look it up," I said aloud. I brushed the ants off and dashed inside to my *Birds of New Mexico*.

"Swallow, violet-green. p. 281."[1] Before I read one word, the photograph itself seemed conclusive. The same pose, the identical angle, the same gorgeous green, the same white, the same dark wings, no visible tail, and no visible violet either. I read on. "Violet blue wings," though in the photo they looked gray, ". . . can be attracted with a nest box." When I read that its wing tips extended beyond the tail whenever it perched, I was engulfed by a powerful sense of certainty that this was Anne. Flooded with unadulterated joy, I ran outside and shouted up into the sky, "I got it, Anne, I got it!" I was infused with this joy all day, though I felt uneasy about this at first. Shouldn't I be grieving? Here my friend had died and all I could feel was joyful? Was I too identified with my researcher/writer self to grieve? As the morning progressed, I came to realize this joy was coming directly from Anne. The story she had told was of a suffering bird, near death, and of its joyful release. Anne had been that suffering bird and now she too had been released, not back into life but onward out of her physical suffering and into death. Even the annoying ants and my beloved bluebirds had conspired to reveal how exactly a plan for after-death connection could be made and manifested. I pondered the precision with which the swallow had mirrored the pose in my bird book, and Anne's orderly, almost scientific, approach to certain issues.

I shared my experience at her memorial service in the meditation building in the meadow at the end of my road, where I heard there had been an unprecedented total of four double rainbows in our neighborhood the week following her death. People spoke of feeling Anne's joy through the rainbows. I heard about a pact she had made to reassure others as a yellow butterfly, of how her son-in-law and one granddaughter had already driven Anne's cat and dog back to live with them, and of the yellow butterfly that kept following her dog in their Wisconsin yard, a thousand miles from Anne's New Mexico home.

☙

I have interviewed quite a few people about after-death contacts made through nature, though nearly all these contacts were spontaneous. I have seen that when the dead visit us in this manner, besides the usual reassurance, they also help us break through our long-held cultural bias that we humans can't have meaningful exchanges with nature. That birds sing among themselves or soar, elks bugle or bound, butterflies flutter and float, and all we get to do is listen and watch. We tend to see ourselves as separate from nature and its language as pretty much indecipherable. Yet look at Findhorn in Scotland, where community members dialogue with nature to rid the gardens of pests and grow phenomenally large vegetables. The biomimicry folks are allowing nature to teach humans its ways for all our benefit. And any tribal culture that has retained its traditional practices communicates with nature continually.

In receiving an ADC through nature we participate in an ancient and venerable tradition. A shamanic counselor told me that, generally and not just with the dead, her clients receive communication through birds more than through any other aspect of nature. Among those I have spoken with, birds have also been nature's most common ADC messengers. Contacts through nature tend to be wordless, yet just as relieving as verbal contact would be. I was told people instantly recognized their dead beloved's presence in a bird (or a butterfly or a dragonfly), and they knew this meant the person was all right.

I originally assumed this frequency of contact via birds was due to their accessibility. Even if we live among high-rises, we can still see birds. Yet when I delved into *The Book of the Dead* I found entire sections of this ancient Egyptian text—originally written in hieroglyphics—devoted to the transformation of the dead into birds—mostly hawks, swallows, and herons. There were hawks of gold, divine hawks, and human-headed hawks. The Egyptians saw the swallow as the precursor of happy news. Closer to home the Native peoples of the Americas revere eagles, hawks, condors, and ravens, which are sometimes called messengers from heaven or visionaries of the air, and their messages are listened to with reverence. You will read later about my own and my granddaughter's ADC experiences with hawks and eagles.

I can't grasp how the dead communicate through these beings, only that they do so. How on earth does a bird or a butterfly become a messenger from the dead? Does Uncle Frank actually transform himself into the bird? Does cousin Mary meld with the consciousness of a butterfly? What does it mean for a butterfly to have consciousness? One guiding principle, or *saywa*, passed down from the ancient Incan people, says, "Everything is interconnected and one." Are the dead simply able to accept their oneness with a bird or butterfly? And does my desire to understand how this works only reflect what Vine Deloria Jr. in his classic *God is Red* calls our modern desire to explain life rather than to experience it?[2]

ॐ

In another vein, it's fairly typical for the dead to attend their own funerals and memorial services. A man who had been unable to walk for some time prior to his death is heard boasting, "I can run now." Another is seen acting as a kind of a greeter, standing by the door as his funeral attendees enter. Ruth Rousseau-Clothier, author of *Keys of Internal Wisdom* and the forthcoming *Wisdom of the Heart: The Book of Life,* shared her experience as a child after the death of a beloved, elderly neighbor. Ruth was so distressed by Mrs. Maloney's death that, despite being only a toddler, she was taken to the wake to help her understand why her friend could not be with her. Her parents showed her the body in the casket, and patiently explained again that Mrs. Maloney had gone to be with God.

"No, she hasn't!"

They explained yet again, "She's not here anymore."

"She is too," Ruth called out. "She is right here." Everyone stared as she pointed toward the foot of the casket, where she could see Mrs. Maloney drawing a heart on her own chest, just as she had frequently done in life, then pointing toward Ruth's heart, and mouthing, "I love you." When Ruth rushed over for a hug, Mrs. Maloney seemed to convey the message that Ruth could "see the truth" and should never close down to it. It is difficult to comprehend that a child of that age could retain these words. Ruth remembers thinking the woman referred to her ability to see this vision. Perhaps if we were to follow the thread from this moment to Ruth's books, we would discover Mrs. Maloney's larger meaning. Much later, Ruth's mother told her that as they embraced, every attendee sobbed, amazed by the child's ability to "see."

I suspect that many more children have this ability than we acknowledge. Ruth's personality allowed her to argue, and what she said and did convinced those around her. Many children are more circumspect; many parents are more dismissive, and children sense disapproval and dismissiveness even if unspoken. In any case, without the support of a culture that accepts such abilities, they tend to fade. I find it helpful to remember that these talents lie dormant within each one of us—not far away at all—awaiting our willingness to accept them, our attention, and the right circumstances.

છ

I heard two eerily alike stories of playing children who had sudden certainty that something had happened—in one case to a father, in the other to a grandfather. In each of the two situations, the children were right, the men had indeed just died. In another case, a ten-year-old boy's bicycle seems suddenly to get "all loose and wobbly," throwing him to the ground. He simply knows his failing grandmother has died at that moment. He collects himself and continues the short ride home on his totally undamaged bicycle. His mother is on the phone being told of his grandmother's death as he arrives. Now this boy is a man, a lawyer who considers himself an atheist, yet he has this memory. "I have no home for it," he tells me, pointing out that he was not even particularly close to this grandmother. Atheist or not, this homeless moment is a seed he carries within him. I wonder if someday another experience may nourish that seed to sprout into increased awareness of life's transcendence.

Chapter Two

TELL FREDDY I'M
NOT MAD AT HIM

A sweet thing, for whatever time,
to revisit in dreams the dear dead we have lost.

—*Euripides,* Alcestis

A dream may be a moment of magic or of madness. Often it is a conundrum, a not easily soluble riddle, yet it is also the road most readily traversed between the transcendent realm and our conscious awareness. We may remember or ignore our dreams, be fearful of or fascinated by them, understand them or feel completely befuddled. We parse them for relevance with psychotherapists. Freudians search for the sexual needle in their haystack. Jungians seek out both the personal and the collective unconscious. Lucid dreamers are aware when they dream, capable of consciously creating what occurs within their dream-state. We dream during the several segments of a night's sleep that are often unimaginatively called REM sleep, after the rapid eye movement that occurs then. I prefer the less common name, "paradoxical sleep," after the paradox that our brains are fully awake while our bodies are so asleep we can be running or dancing in a dream without kicking our partners or falling out of bed.

Like poetry, dreams often don't reveal their richness without our active participation. That's why there are so many dream interpretation dictionaries, dream study groups, dream magazines and books, organizations like the International Association for the Study of Dreams. Not that I recommend all of these. Dream dictionaries, for instance, can tell us what a fig leaf meant to Freud or a buffalo to a Navajo, but no one else can tell me what these mean in my dream. Like magicians we need to pull the rabbit out of our own dream hats. In my dream group, based on Jeremy Taylor's work, we use the phrase, "If this were my dream . . ." to preface responses to someone else's dream. It is a phrase that originated with Montague Ullman and was popularized by Taylor, author of the delightfully titled, *When People Fly and Water Runs Uphill*. We go on to state what the dream would have meant to *us* if we had had it. Hearing several such reflections gives me fresh insight into what the transcendent is trying to get through my sometimes very thick skull. Most of us dream of those we love when they are alive and frequently we continue to dream of them after their deaths. Not all of these are ADC dreams, though many of them very definitely are. Patricia Garfield and Robert Moss have both written entire books focused on ADC dreams.

A peculiar mood enveloped me as I worked on this chapter. Since the dreams themselves were so uplifting to write about, I could not fathom why I was rising from my desk every day as if surrounded by a dark cloud. This caused me to correlate my research in a fresh way, until I found my answer. It is a given that deaths generally sadden us, but there are certain deaths, the ones most often called tragic or traumatic, that are even more of a challenge for the living. These may involve a young person, or the death may be sudden. There is the shock of accident or violence. There may be estrangement, unfinished business, addiction, a sense of a wasted life, scant chance to heal the wounded parts of a relationship, or a self-inflicted death. These deaths can leave us unable to function at all. There are those—mothers in particular—who never recover from such losses, with the wound festering and infecting the rest of a life. About half of those I have interviewed have had significant after-death contact with dead beloveds through dreams. What I discovered at this point was that among these more difficult deaths, fully 75 percent of the contacts were through dreams. It was writing about this preponderance of tragedy that had so troubled me, reminding me once again of the potent effect of after-death contact to give succor when it is most needed. Besides their vividness, the key distinction in ADC dreams is their ability to transport us into new understandings that may bring profound healing. They are particularly effective in easing our struggles with these most traumatic deaths.

ల

My mother's death did not fit this traumatic pattern. She was sixty-nine and had had cancer for a year; her death was expected. My father, however, died sixteen days later with little warning. This second death was made enormously more challenging by both its suddenness and its proximity to the first. My sister Eve and I were desolate, and that desolation was laced with emotions I'm less than proud of—resentment tinged with anger. The cause of our father's death was unclear. We agreed to an autopsy, but to us it seemed that he had chosen to abandon us for our mother just when we needed him the most. Then I had my first ADC dream. My mother had been an accomplished ballroom dancer, but because of my father's childhood polio, he walked with canes. So they had never danced together. More recently, post-polio syndrome had weakened my father's shoulders and arms as well. Here is what I came to call "the" dream:

I am in a huge, elegant, and shadowy ballroom. A live orchestra plays a Strauss waltz. The parquet floor gleams. A couple circles in graceful loops. As they near me, I recognize my father in a dark suit. My mother's gown spreads its bias-cut, silvery satin skirt in a wide arc on each spin. I call out, "Mother! Daddy!" I wave. They don't respond. "I'm over here." I step into their path. "It's me!" They dance around me. No matter what I do, they remain focused only on each other, their faces a study in love.

Had this been an ordinary dream, I might have awakened with my sense of abandonment heightened; after all, my parents had completely ignored me. Instead, my grief had softened, and I felt the first faint inkling of peace. I could even see some right order in their waltz with death, my mother stepping backward into its arms, my father following. For the first time I could accept that my father's death was about something besides me. I don't know if I wrote this dream down, yet I can still see my mother's dress as clearly as if I had seen it last night. The reason this dream remains with such clarity is that how I was before it and how I was after it were not the same. I have had dreams, sweet or painful, of my parents since, but this is the one I can write from memory thirty years later.

Soon my sister Eve had a dream, too, in which she and our father sat opposite one another at a conference table in an airplane cleared of its other seats. Eve said, "I don't understand why you had to die." He replied that he had been experiencing *wing-longing*. Here was a man with paralyzed legs who had spent his life using his muscular arms to walk with canes. When those arms weakened, why wouldn't he long for wings? Eve too awoke from her dream with her grief and resentment softened, as mine had been. Sharing these dreams with each other enhanced their transformative effect. This is a typical result of ADC dreams, in that we were both moved from Point A to Point B overnight.

Eve later dreamed of our parents, younger, vibrant, and dressed up as she had loved to see them, our father in his fedora, our mother in the orange-flowered dress and matching necklace and earrings that had been Eve's favorite outfit. As they spoke, their bodies expanded and collapsed, then puffed up again like balloons. When she asked, "What do you think of President Reagan?" Mother's reply was, We don't think about those things here. Note how the dead prioritize life differently than we do, as in when a woman dreams of telling her deceased mother she wished she had done more to ease the process of her dying—an issue that had been really bothering her. Her mother's response—When did that happen?—makes her daughter's concern seem totally irrelevant.

৩১

Viewing life and death as journeys helps to clarify why travel and trains and boats and planes appear so often in dreams with the dead. Doris' deceased father told her, I just want to let you know I'm okay, and then boarded a train that headed off into darkness. Terry's daughter showed up on a ship. Emily's father came to her after his death, while her mother was still living, to say, I love you and I miss you. Your mom and I are going on a trip soon and this may be the last time you see us, which gave her some preparatory warning of her mother's impending death. In one of the occasional dreams I've had with my daughter Randi, we were on an airplane, with a skewed aspect because, though we each had an empty seat beside us, I sat in a row behind her. I took this to mean that as I journey through life, though our next destination—death—is the same, she is ahead of me.

৩১

I met Darleen when I was invited to speak at a support group for those whose beloveds had died by suicide. A look of recognition crossed her face when I mentioned the vivid, unforgettable quality of ADC dreams, but she said nothing in the group. Others shared ADC experiences that evening in confidence, so they cannot be included here, but Darleen and I arranged to speak later. In the interview Darleen told me that writing down the travel dream she had had several years after her teenage daughter's suicide was "almost like taking dictation."

In this dream, the family was preparing for a vacation, though her daughter, Kama, would drive herself to a different locale to camp out "under the stars." After the dream vacation had begun, Darleen sensed Kama was short on money, so she took a side trip to give her more. Darleen and Kama communicated without words, which were unnecessary. Since Darleen rarely remembers her dreams, this one stands out. It has continued to feed her over time, as she made the connection between the small detail of Kama camping out under the stars and the poem about stars found in Kama's journal and read at her funeral.

Darleen called this a "culmination" dream, saying it was pivotal to her transformation "from all-consuming grief to letting her go. My emotion at the end was relief, with Kama glad to be managing on her own." This allowed Darleen to return her attention to her husband and her two other children, thus having an "indirect healing effect" on the entire family.

Besides travel, a pertinent pattern in Darleen's dream is that of giving money to her daughter. Another mother had a series of two dreams that included this theme. In the first one, her adult son drew a picture of her being completely under water. When she awoke from this dream, she told her husband, "Something terrible has happened." That morning they received the call that their son had drowned. A couple of weeks later, deep in the grieving process, she dreamed her son was walking by as she sat in a café. There was a river nearby. He stopped and asked her for money for the ferry to cross the river. Just as Darleen had done, she gave her son money.

In ancient Greece it was Charon who ferried the dead across the River Styx into the Elysian Fields. Since a fee was required for this ferry, before burial, coins were placed on the dead, under their tongues or between their teeth, or on their lips or eyelids, or in their hands. So the practice of giving the dead money for the journey across has historical and mythological significance. It also seems significant that both these dreamers are mothers; giving money to our children implies parental support and, perhaps, a certain acknowledgment of their new state.

∽

The next small group of dreams falls on the periphery of the classic healing after-death communication dream. Each one arrived closely on the heels of a death. They were given to me as ADC dreams. They were with beloveds. They were vivid and they have stayed strong in the dreamers' memories, but they were less than satisfying and neither brought nor displayed transformation.

When Willa began her story, I was intrigued by her description of her mother as an artist, into yoga and the

Self-Realization Fellowship and Yogananda's teachings. But Willa went on to say that her mother had often spoken of death as freedom from life's struggles, that she had been "too perfunctory to be a good mother" and perhaps had never wanted children. Willa had this dream three days after her mother's death. In it she ran toward her mother, who was "doing acrobatic flips in the firmament, literally dancing with the stars," with a joyful attitude that proclaimed, "I'm free of everything." Willa's arms were open and outstretched, but her mother did not embrace her, and Willa was left as dissatisfied as ever. It seemed to her that she was part of what her mother was so glad to be free of.

Two other dreamers shared similar dreams they'd had within days of a death. On the night of his death, a woman who had taken away her eighty-two-year-old alcoholic father's car to keep him and others on the road safe, dreamed of him standing beside his car, gloating that now he had it back. On the night a man's grandmother burned to death in her home, along with her collection of valuable Navajo weavings, he vividly dreamed of her and his dead grandfather, who had come to say goodbye. She stood amid the ashes of her home, holding her face in her hands and bemoaning, What's happened to all my stuff? These three people have yet to release their tight hold on their points of view, their cars, their weavings—their "stuff." Death had not yet brought transformation, so the dreams did not shift the dreamers into new understandings.

Yvonne's experience—not a dream—happened within a few days of her father's death and reflects the same early, pre-transformative stage. She and her brother were rearranging some of their father's belongings when they heard a thunderous banging in the "attic" above them. This was confusing, since the house had no attic, and almost at once Yvonne thought this must be her father, angry at having his possessions moved around. In Patricia Garfield's book on dreaming with the dead she relates a dream in which a mother is angry at her children for sorting through her closet right away; a later dream brought forgiveness for this.[1] Yvonne's father also did not hold on to his anger. As she slept beside her mother in "his spot," he patted her hand, "as if he were letting me know everything was okay." This seems to demonstrate the need for pause following a death—for prayer and ritual, taking a deep breath—before normal activity is resumed.

Because of our modern, mostly medical, take on death, we are encouraged to perceive it as a one-step process. One moment we are alive and breathing, our heart beats, our blood flows; in the next those functions have stopped, and a doctor proclaims an official moment of death. Another way to view death is that it can be a gradual process more than an event. Often dying people close down to the physical slowly over hours or days. They may lose interest in talk, touch, food, weather. They often see or speak with beloveds who have predeceased them that no one else can see or hear. After bodily functions cease, the transition may still continue. This is why, for instance, for three days post-death Tibetan Buddhists touch the body as little as possible and pray over it, allowing the transition to continue undisturbed. In the three dreams I have just shared, this transition is not yet complete.

If dreams we have right away are less than satisfying, it seems best not to give them too much weight.

☙

At times our dead beloveds come into our dreams with messages for someone else that can have enormous positive impact. Human thinking tends to be divisive, *my* body, *your* body, *my* psyche, *your* dreams. Receiving messages for another allows us to step outside ourselves to a vantage point where we may see that—like the cells of our bodies—besides being unique, we are also aspects of a single and interconnected whole.

Children's book author and illustrator Lisa was twelve when her grandmother died. They had been close, and that closeness continued when Lisa had the following dream. Tell Freddy I'm not mad at him, her grandmother directed, sitting beside a man Lisa did not recognize. When she told Freddy, who was her father, this dream, he burst into tears. Unbeknownst to Lisa, her father was suffering within a deep well of guilt. His mother had asked him never to put her into a nursing home, but following her stroke, he had needed to do just that. As if to underscore the veracity of this message, when Lisa described the man in her dream to her father, he told her, "That's your grandfather," who had died when Lisa was two. By her grandmother sending this message through her, not only was Freddy relieved of his burden of guilt, but twelve-year-old Lisa was taught something about interconnectedness and the power of dreaming and her father's emotional life.

A dream directed Emily to deliver a message to the daughter of a deceased man she had known only slightly, but Emily worried about how strangely the message—and the messenger—might be received. She barely knew the daughter, although she did know where she worked. Emily screwed up her nerve and went there. As she waited in line, she continued to vacillate about delivering the message. Arriving at Nina's desk, she plunged ahead with her tale, ending with, "Your father asked me to tell you, I'm fine and I'm happy." Just as Freddy had done, Nina burst into tears, sobbing out, "This is precisely what I needed to hear." We don't know why Nina received this message through another person. Had her father attempted to tell his daughter himself and simply not gotten through? Or was it because by using Emily as a messenger, two people could be affected at one time? For Emily, taking the risk to trust and to act on her dream's direction and having its message be so well received was a confirmation. Each time we trust a dream's guidance, we build up our dream-state's ability to play a stronger role in supporting us.

ↀ

For an ADC dream to be memorable requires neither messages nor complexity. Brevity can be the soul not only of wit, but of a satisfying contact. As when Kerry's dad, appearing fit and handsome in a white business suit, slips into her brother's swimming pool with her and says, It's okay. It's all right. Or when a woman's adult son taps her on the shoulder and, when she turns around, motions toward his outfit, Mom, check out the robes. He seems to be reminding her to lighten up, perhaps the hardest challenge for a mother. Other dreams are even more simple, though often equally as memorable: a kiss on the lips or a long and satisfying hug.

⁓

What lingers after a death, the memory of an emaciated body or a face full of pain, can be terribly disturbing. We may be unable to rid ourselves of the sight and sound of ICU monitoring equipment, the beeps of an IV bag needing to be changed. The shock of the death itself can override all the pleasant memories of life with this beloved person. After-death communication can take on the task of dispelling or replacing these disturbing memories.

Diane and her childhood friend had both grown up into alcoholism, and later they had both become sober. Diane stayed that way. Her friend, though she sobered up again and again, could never make it stick, and eventually drink destroyed her. After her friend's death, Diane was furious at her—"One thing to do with grief"—she told me. She could not recall the simplest of her dear friend's characteristics. In a dream, Diane telephoned her. Because she was aware in the dream that her friend had died, it almost surprised her that she picked up the phone. As they spoke, Diane got to hear her happy and familiar voice and laughter. That laughter seemed the most gratifying, and the quality that remains most deeply embedded in her memory now.

⁓

The librarian at our new local library placed my flyer in the star spot inside the front door, but the only person who responded to that particular flyer was Earl, a teacher and a writer. I got the sense he was puzzled that I wanted to meet with him, instead of just hearing his dream right there and then on the phone, but I count on the intimacy of face-to-face interviews to enhance the communication. We pulled our lawn chairs into the dappled sunlight by the creek that rushes behind his canyon home. His face clouded over as he told me about his old friend, how they had been close years earlier and then drifted apart as his friend turned to alcohol and cocaine and a "dissipated lifestyle." Now they were both in their sixties, yet in the dream his friend was "clear, like a young divinity student." They did not speak in the dream, but this changed appearance convinced Earl that his friend was dead, which a phone call to his friend's wife later confirmed.

Being told of a death through a dream, either before it would be possible to learn of it or, as in Earl's situation, when we might not be informed through external means, is not unusual. Over dinner in the bougainvillea-draped courtyard of La Jicara, one of my favorite Oaxacan restaurants, Juanita, an eighty-year-old Mexican psychotherapist who still practices part-time, shared the dream she had as she traveled through Europe. Her friend had been having heart problems before she left. In this dream he seemed to say, "Let's keep in touch," nothing more, yet this was enough to make her wonder if he had died. She found out her intuition was true on her return home. This dream's simple message of a friend's desire to maintain connection was dear to Juanita. I love how the dead make these little tips of the hat on the way out of their bodies, letting us know that separation, distance, and lifestyle choices have little significance in the larger scheme of our connected existence.

ℰↄ

Though I have not dreamed often with Randi, my husband Spencer's contact with his stepdaughter has all been through dreams. He speaks of the following two with such gratitude it leans toward reverence. Not long after Randi's death he dreamed that he and I and my daughter Rowena and her son Ollin were sharing a meal when Spencer returned to the restaurant's plant-filled entryway. He stood contemplating the water flowing in a lovely fountain in an alcove on the wall. When we joined him there, he told us, "Randi has just landed," and awoke relieved of his fear that her suicide might have prevented her from crossing safely over.

In the second dream, a couple of months later, he and I and Randi's daughter Chelsey had been invited to Randi's new home in the country. First she showed us the open-sided gazebo surrounded by greenery and trees where she said she loved to sleep. This especially pleased him because of its dissimilarity to how she had confined herself to her stale and airless bedroom in the depths of her depression. It gave him a sense that she was progressing. She directed us to the front door of her house. As if to illustrate the differences between the living and the dead, she entered another way, and let us all in from inside. The spacious, light-filled house was mostly empty, except for numerous animal-motif decorative objects on its white walls. He wondered to me why she was already decorating the walls, while the house had so little furniture. About the time he had this dream, Randi told me in a visitation that she spent most of her time "in healing." I wanted to know more. She did not explain, but since she was in a healing process, I envisioned her with little need for more than a bed, beautiful surroundings, and reminders of her beloved animals. After this dream Spencer realized it wasn't necessary to understand her suicide, only to accept that now she was all right.

ೞ

At the start of my interview with Terry, though we each knew the other had a daughter who had died, we did not know that the cause of both deaths had been suicide. Once this was revealed, there was much to share, and much that did not need to be said at all. His daughter was buried on her twentieth birthday. Months later he dreamed of being with her on a ship, where she showed him how she was orienting newly dead suicides. This is how I pay back what I have done, she told her father.

Why pay back? I wondered. Payback smacks to me of the concept of suicide as sin that some people propound. Long before Randi's death, the idea of considering an action as sad as suicide to be a sin did not resonate well with me. That loaded word *sin* did not enter into what hypnotherapist Michael Newton found in his research on what occurs between lives. In his book, *Destiny of Souls,* Newton writes of suicides with young, healthy bodies wasting life's gift of opportunity.[2] Perhaps it is that sense of wasted opportunity that this young suicide was expiating on that ship in her father's dream.

Terry went on to tell me about a series of dreams he had had long ago. After his mother abandoned the family when he was a child, his oldest sister became his surrogate mother until her death in a car accident when Terry was twenty-three. Terry dreamed again and again of family reunions with all of his siblings and their mother. He clung to mourning his sister, keeping their connection alive through his deep suffering. After twenty years of this, his sister shouted at him in a dream, You are holding me back. Stop it! His mourning stopped on the spot. He says he had nothing to do with this cessation; it was simply his natural response to new understanding to turn away from self-pity. This is the power the dead have to transform a twenty-year-old pattern in a heartbeat.

☙

Dreams are the nucleus of Anna and Steve Racicot's lives. They dream prolifically and sometimes lucidly and often greet the day by sharing dreams. They have founded several dream groups, including the one my husband and I participate in. In the 1990s they began publishing *Night Vision: A Dream Journal*, which would run for five years. Naturally, when their friend Irene died, they both dreamed of her. During the final segment of Irene's life, Anna and Irene had not gotten along quite as well as they had before. After Irene's death at age ninety-six, Anna dreamed of her friend cleaning house and clearing out what she did not want, and Anna and Steve sandwiched her in a long, healing hug. This single dream, Anna says, "returned us to the core of our loving relationship," a phrase I've heard repeated nearly word-for-word about the healing effect of several kinds of after-death connection. In this same dream, Anna asked whether Irene owned her home, but Irene seemed confused by the question. Perhaps ownership has no reality in the afterlife?

When Steve dreamed of Irene, she looked sixty and perky and happy. She told him she had revived . . . had recovered. Sixty is the youngest he would have easily recognized her, since they had met when she was in her sixties. The age of the dead in an ADC dream often flexes. Almost invariably they look younger and healthier than when last seen, but how much younger seems to be determined by what is needed to facilitate recognition. A grown son or daughter might appear as twenty or thirty, when they had looked in their prime. Yet if we dream of a parent, since we might not recognize them in their prime, they are more likely to come as forty or fifty or sixty, though still younger and healthier. An exception to this is Lenore's mother who was young in a dream image Lenore could recognize from a familiar family photo. In Darleen's dream, her daughter, who had died at fourteen, was now old enough to drive, this maturing a pleasing detail to her mother.

ℰℐ

One service that can occur in dreams is that of escorting someone safely across into the realm of the dead, which is sometimes called psychopomp work. The word *psychopomp* comes from the Greek terms *psyche* (breath, life, soul, mind) and *pompos* (conductor or guide). There are many myths and beliefs about those who do this service, including the Greek god Hermes and the Egyptian jackal-headed god Anubis. In Christianity this is often the work of the angels, especially Archangel Michael. The Boddhisattva Jiso is a Buddhist psychopomp. In Islam, Azrael, the angel of death, escorts the dead across. In traditional cultures it is the shaman who ensures that the soul crosses over safely.

Now there are modern shamanic practitioners available for this work called death midwives, deathwalkers, or spiritual counselors. Catholics and some Anglicans pray the Novena for various numbers of days or weeks to assist in this transition. When my Tibetan Buddhist friend Anne died, lamas, fellow practitioners, and friends prayed over her body for three days and gathered again for specific prayers on both the seventh and the forty-ninth day following her death. Mexican filmmaker Francisco Athic's *Vera* portrays a surreal and exquisite fictionalized version of this time-honored service, complete with "Vera" as guide and a boat for crossing the river. Anna Racicot dreamed of her deceased mother escorting a dear acquaintance into death, except that in her dream it wasn't a river they crossed but Anna's clothesline. Even with that roguish dream turn, she awakened sure this old friend had died. Soon her father sent the man's obituary, confirming his death.

❧

Luis, who excavated the foundation for my home, has performed spontaneous psychopomp work a number of times in his dreams. He does this service without benefit of the knowledge death brings, which Anna's mother had, or of training or of having a highfalutin' Greek-originated name for it either. Like many local Hispanics—*Norteños* as we sometimes say here in northern New Mexico—his family descends from the original settlers who arrived from Spain via Mexico more than four hundred years ago. Luis lives surrounded by relatives on land that has been in his family for generations, and he often dreams of his relatives and his ancestors. Some are elders he barely recalls; some died long before his birth. I wonder if his unusual dreaming skill stems from his family's sustained connection with the land where he lives.

At a large family gathering in a dream, his maternal grandfather tells him, "It's time to take me." They get into a truck and Luis drives his grandfather over a hill, returning to the party alone, where everyone knows his grandfather has died, yet no one is sad. In another dream, Luis and all his uncles are in a meadow with aspen trees just before sunrise. There are rays or beams of celestial music sung by angels. These beams of song bring the morning light, which gets brighter and brighter. Then Luis walks one uncle over the hill, once again returning without him. In each case, the relative died shortly after his dream. Whenever he has this kind of dream, his body is bathed in warmth throughout the next day. This sensation, he says, is so real it's like receiving a long hug.

Once, wrestling with a difficult decision, he turned his face upward as if looking for an answer in the sky. The clouds parted to reveal a vision of his dead grandmother's radiant face. She did not speak, yet, as though directed, he went immediately to the nearby cemetery where so many of his family members have been buried. Among the remains of his ancestors, he sobbed and sobbed until he had made his tough decision. Another time, Luis was driving his backhoe to repair a problem on his deceased uncle's land and kept turning around, sure someone was watching him. After a few times of this, he was finally able to see his uncle behind him giving him the support and gratitude of a repeated thumbs-up sign while Luis continued to work. Each of these experiences was followed by that extended feeling of a warm embrace.

Usually psychopomp service is done at the time of death or afterward, not as Luis has done, prior to the deaths, so why is the timing this way in his dreams? In the transcendent realms, time as we know it does not exist. Numerous men and women of wisdom say that transcendent time is simply "now"—a realm where past, present, and future coexist. We may experience this state when we are so involved in an activity we lose all awareness of time. In earth-time, Luis' uncle and grandfather were still alive. In now-time their deaths were already visible and present while they still lived. In now-time Luis could give them his support a little bit in advance, perhaps to ease their minds as they approached their deaths, to prepare them to find the path, just as the dreams prepare him for the deaths that were about to come.

℘

Hal, now a mature, articulate, and confident man, told me a story that began years ago when he and his closest friend Donnie were young rock musicians. Donnie, their band's leader and drummer and a poet and a guitarist, was forever talking about spiritual matters, though he couldn't drum up much interest among the "crazy, beer-drinking" band members.

One day, as Hal and Donnie played Frisbee with their dogs, Donnie broke off the game to go mow his parents' lawn. He declined Hal's offer of help, and Hal never saw Donnie alive again. He was killed when he cut through the electric cord of his parents' hedge clippers as he stood on the sopping wet lawn he had just watered. For twenty-one-year-old Hal this was an appalling loss. His distress was magnified by the poem he found propped up on Donnie's snare drum. Donnie had never left a poem there before. This one was titled "Signing Off," and it was all about leaving, checking out, signing off. It unleashed a maelstrom of questions within Hal. Had Donnie known he was about to die? Had he wanted to die? Could he even have deliberately cut that cord to take his own life? This death and the questions it raised began a new cycle of Hal's life during which he repeatedly dreamed the same dream in which he and Donnie greeted one another like the good friends they were, but Donnie was always sad. He always carried his guitar, and he always told Hal he was sad because he could not play his guitar without his body.

This seems clearly a circumstance in which Donnie was unable to cross over. Sudden accidental deaths sometimes confuse people in this way, leaving them stranded and in need of guidance. Hal recalls having this dream about a dozen times over a ten-year period. The questions that had arisen when Donnie died did not leave him. Instead they expanded into ever-larger questions about life and death and spirit, and especially about dreams. Hal became a lucid dreamer, so capable of dream recall that for fifteen years he wrote down five or ten dreams every night. A decade after Donnie's death, Hal had his final Donnie dream. This time Donnie stood happily at a crossroads. He told Hal, I'm leaving now, and walked on down the road.

There are many ways to view Donnie's death and the dreams that followed it. First, I'm going to assume that his death was accidental. It is not unusual, particularly in the case of sudden, accidental deaths like this one, for behaviors preceding those deaths to reveal a level of foreknowledge. I suspect it's not that Donnie wrote the poem consciously aware he was about to die, but that it bubbled to the surface from that part of him that did know. And that part guided his hand to leave the poem where Hal would find it. Donnie did not cross over into death completely; he clung tightly— for an entire decade—to his physical body and his physical guitar, perhaps still not fully aware that he had died. This is exactly the situation that psychopomp work can heal or prevent. To me, in my time-bound life, ten years is a hideously long time to wander between the worlds. I yearn for Donnie to have been released from that trap immediately. From another perspective, it may be that in the timeless state this was only a flash to Donnie, like when we cut a finger and cry out and in a moment the pain is gone. To Hal, living in a physical body, the decade-long recurring dream reminder of his important questions may have been the most generous gift his dear friend could have offered. Perhaps it was even the primary purpose for their brief friendship.

At the end of our interview, Hal spoke of how this series of dreams had helped him to recognize when he was in the land of the dead, of holding long, rich conversations with an uncle who had been severely retarded; that the part of his uncle's brain that had been damaged in the birth canal was no longer needed in death, where consciousness, not the brain, is the tool for communication. Hal has taught himself to move consciously, via his breath, into the hypnagogic[3] state just before sleep, which he calls "the fountain of knowledge."

ↅↄ

As you can tell by this selection of dreams, it would be a stretch to say there are typical after-death communication dreams. The most we can claim is that they sometimes contain repeated patterns or threads, such as travel or messages. These dreams are precisely tailored by some synergy of spirit, and the dead who live within spirit, or by that part of us that lives within spirit, to fit our idiosyncratic needs to perfection, unlike the wide gulfs of misunderstanding in communication that can occur between living human beings.

The same dream dreamed by another might seem an enigma, yet *we* get it. Out of the context of my mother's ballroom dancing and my father's polio, the dancing dream I began this chapter with is merely a charming, if uncomfortable, scene. Would dreaming of an old friend looking "clear—like a young divinity student" trigger you to know he was dead? Would dreaming of a helping hand over a clothesline convince you of a death?

Chapter Three

LIKE A GURU IN
MY POCKET

All goes onward and outward, nothing collapses,
And to die is different from what any one supposed,
and luckier.

Has any one supposed it lucky to be born?
I hasten to inform him or her it is just as lucky to die,
and I know it.
—Walt Whitman, "Song of Myself"

Annie: Is contact between the living and the dead a problem for the dead?

Randi: On the soul level, that is, when we come as soul to soul, there is
no longing for the dead to be living, there is no pull, no draw back to
the earth plane, so it's okay. If contact is made through too much pain,
that can be detrimental to the dead. If the living can accept the dead as
we are, then contact is sweet and satisfying to both, as our contact is.

Annie: Is it hard for you to contact me?

Randi: It takes energy, but not that much, because you come so far toward me. What's hard is getting others to notice that I am with them.

Annie: I sense that you're with me a lot of the time, even when we're not in conversation. Is that true?

Randi: I am.

Annie: Is that a good thing? I feel a little uneasy about it.

Randi: The dead are among the living a lot. You just happen to be aware of it with me.

Our deceased beloveds are amazingly intentional and wise in their contact with us. I know from my reading that repeated and ongoing verbal contact has happened to many besides myself. Yet among those I have interviewed, no one else has had so much verbal contact they needed to establish a special notebook to track it. When my grief overwhelmed me and my energy for this project lagged, Randi urged me so strongly to refocus, it was obvious how much she wanted this book to manifest. Those of us who feel called to share our after-death contact, mostly via books, though now there are also blogs and other online means for sharing, receive extraordinary help and support from our dead beloveds. Randi told me, People need to talk of these things, to hear and read about them, to KNOW.

Sometimes the intention of the dead is to communicate information about the afterlife. Randi, however, focused almost exclusively on various ways to illustrate after-death communication itself. It's as though she worked her way through a checklist of ADC types. She has come to me as both an external voice (though only the first time) and an internal one, and through my body. She has mucked with electricity. She has come to her stepfather in dreams, to her daughter and to me through nature and in a synchronous experience, to her father in a vision, to a friend as an undeniable presence that directed her to find out about Randi's death, and to her sister through someone who looked just like her. I am left wondering if the willingness of those like myself to write and to speak of our contact encourages the disembodied to speak, so we become their voices here in the land of the living.

Besides the writing of this book, Randi told me the purpose of our contact was to heal the differences between the two of us, as well as to support her daughter Chelsey. I had more inclusive ideas originally, because our contact stirred up my curiosity. Here was my chance to explore death with someone having firsthand experiences. I wanted to know everything about where she was. Though I peppered her with questions, I now know little more about the afterlife than before I asked. When I asked if our contact could help her with her suffering, the tone of her reply—No, that's being taken care of here—firmly closed the door on the subject of how this transformation was happening. When I asked her what it was like where she was, she replied that it was peaceful and a place of healing without further explanation. When I was reading about spirit guides and asked her what she could tell me about them, she said nothing at all.

Annie: Are you going to answer?
Randi: No.

Annie: Why not?

Randi: There are limitations to this communication.

Annie: So it's not the purpose of this connection to give me a full understanding of the other side?

Randi: Right.

If I pushed against these limitations, she turned away. Since I longed for her presence, I quickly learned to honor her boundaries. For this reason, some of our exchanges seemed truncated; there was less back and forth than you and I might have in conversation. Nevertheless her peaceful, gentle presence and guidance granted me a sense of the afterlife. Of course, this only came from her particular vantage point. There may be as many ways to experience death as there are to experience life. Her view is only one tiny window onto a vast landscape. But it is one window, and it does have a view.

When she spoke to me, especially when she spoke at length, her meaning arrived in a kind of a clump. I had to thread this clump through the needle's eye of my mind to divide it into finite words. Even my own thoughts and questions went out to her in a more amorphous manner than when you and I talk. It was almost like a breathing in and breathing out of thoughts and ideas. At times I felt concern I might be contaminating her thoughts with my own.

Annie: Sometimes I think this is just me talking.

Randi: It is. On the soul level you and I are seamless, as we all are, so this contact is from the "I and I" as the Rastafarians say, the many I's where we are the one I.

To touch so closely up against awareness of all our interconnectedness was exhilarating, which made her visitations energizing, yet long ones wore me out, perhaps due to the effort required to bring her meaning into words.

"Are there teachers?" I once queried.

Yes, but I spend most of my time in healing. Again, she gave me no word on how. When I expressed my concern that our visits might interfere with whatever her own tasks were, she replied, Mom, you don't understand. That's human thinking. I can be with you and with Chelsey and with Rowena and doing my own work all at once. We don't have those limitations here. Still, I continued to wonder whether ADC might interfere with what she and, by inference, all the dead need to do. Wanting to be absolutely positive my maternal desire for continued connection would in no way hold my daughter back, I reframed my question to be about my friends Susan and Jesse. They are the couple I wrote about who continued to pretty much cohabit for years after Jesse's death. I asked Randi if this kind of constant connection could keep him from progressing. Not changing her story, she replied, In the largest, timeless realms, if both beings choose, there is no harm done. Their mutuality is the key. Theirs is not a pull from the earth realm only, but a coming together by mutual choice.

About six months after Randi's death, I suddenly sank under a fresh tidal wave of grief, and her visitations stopped cold. I was convinced we would never have contact again. I rode the wave, returned to shore, battered but still breathing, and one morning I felt her blessed presence tingling up my left side. I asked her why she had stayed away so long. You needed to grieve and your comfort must come from the earth plane, she replied.

When I wrote this contact down, I was surprised to see it had been only thirteen days between visitations, not the many weeks it had felt like. I'm sure my emotional state would have been too much of a pull for her. This strikes me as another manifestation of her wisdom, or of the wisdom of the dead in general. They won't come to us if it would do anyone harm.

It seems we must not tug too hard on the sleeve of the dead. Perhaps the fact that I had been so aware of my daughter's suffering when she had been alive has enabled me to receive her presence without too much tugging. I sense that she guards against both tugging on me (so I can heal and go on), and the potential that my tug could drain her energy. I wonder if there is some subtle rhythm to the exchanges between the living and the dead that must occur in order to ensure that ongoing contact is beneficial to both. My interviewee Helena, said of all this, "We call out to the dead, and at some point we need to release the call."

Initially all Randi's visitations were during my early morning hypnopompic state, that neither-here-nor-there land that lies between sleeping and waking that I have always loved. This is when I am least sullied by mental chatter and daily flack. I have a practice of writing a dream intention—about whatever issue seems most pressing—in my dream notebook before sleep. Occasionally this issue finds resolution in a dream; sometimes I have no dream recall at all; often I simply awaken knowing the answer, or a decision makes itself as I lie half-awake in the bed in the morning. It made sense to me that this time would be when I would be most available to engage with my daughter.

After a few months however, Randi's visits moved from my bed to my altar, where I go in the early morning to do an eclectic conglomeration of practices I call my spirit-work. One morning I felt that sweet familiar rush of goose bumps up my left side just as I was starting my mantra practice. I asked if we could wait to talk until afterward. To my surprise, she replied, I come for the mantras. Afterward she explained that, The mantras have an effect on the world. There is a lot of heavy energy . . . sadness, fear, violence. This is draining. Prayers and mantras are uplifting.

The value of prayer arose again when I interviewed Anna, who spoke of her Buddhist teacher's emphasis on prayers for the recently dead. After his own death, as she prayed for him, he manifested in her inner vision during meditation with deep gratitude for her prayers, confirming the value of his own teaching. In *Testimony of Light,* Helen Greaves' book of transcriptions from a deceased friend, the mechanism for this is attributed to how intimately linked the recently dead still are to this plane, their lives, their dear ones, allowing them to receive prayerful intention more readily.[1]

When the news of my daughter's suicide surged out through our various interlocking circles of family and friends, I was told of prayers being said for her and for us in four countries and four languages and at minimum half a dozen spiritual traditions. Catholics said novenas. Cousins from the Jewish branch of our family had a tree planted in Israel in her name. I became convinced these prayers and prayerful actions had helped me to survive. Later I came to wonder how significant a role these prayers played in enabling Randi herself to move to a place of peace so rapidly.

My exchanges with her covered many topics. Some were pragmatic, like help with the details of her estate. She sent messages through me to family members. When I worried about Chelsey, Randi urged me not to, reminding me to allow Chelsey to make her own mistakes. There was one exception to this pattern when Chelsey was planning a trip with friends and Randi stated unequivocally, I do not want Chelsey to drive to Florida. She implied great risk or danger, yet I couldn't clarify specifics. Chelsey seemed nonplussed when I told her this, but when the excursion seemed to fall apart of its own accord and she made plane reservations, Randi expressed her intense gratitude. What had the danger been? The friends? The car? Averting an accident? Avoiding the many tornadoes that hit the middle of the country that summer? I may never know, but it was reassuring to realize we had Randi's support and protection.

Occasionally Randi's former medical field enters into our contact. When I went to an energy healer, Randi rejoiced. I am a doctor, she reminded me, but I can only work with energy now, and I can work with this woman. Did I hear regret in her tone? Did she miss doctoring as much as I missed her medical advice when she had been alive? There was a chapter in this book, where I got particularly mired in the details of the rough draft. Using a medical metaphor, Randi urged me to move on and return to that chapter later. She compared the book to a fetus, which doesn't perfect one hand or the liver before starting to work on the heart or the brain; it develops as an organic whole. Once more I felt our seamlessness. It may be clichéd, but metaphorically all my creative projects are my babies, though

I'm sure I had never mentioned that to her. Who better to midwife this book than my ob-gyn daughter? When I awoke in the middle of one night quite ill, I soon felt her presence rippling slowly and repeatedly through my body. I drifted back to sleep. In the morning I felt fine. When I asked her if she could heal, she replied, I come with the light. It does heal.

Initially Randi would not address anything related to her depression or her suicide. A few months after her death, in the ribbon aisle of a fabric store, I found myself repeatedly excusing myself and squeezing past a woman and her cart. She was in the way and not moving, and I was annoyed with her, until I looked more carefully and noticed how she was pressed back against the display, folded in on herself, staring fixedly at the floor. I asked if she was all right; she shook her head. "Do you need help?" She nodded and painfully squeaked out—"pan-ic"—and, several forced breaths later, "at-tack." We left her filled cart behind as she allowed me to lead her out of the store.

The next morning, Randi, who always seems to know what is happening to me, used this experience to illustrate her former depressed state of consciousness. Inside I felt like that, frozen, unable to move. Do you see why I had to go? I was becoming more and more immobilized. These words, in combination with the level of terror I had felt from this woman, carried me into the core of Randi's suffering. This was horribly painful but so revelatory I could only feel grateful. No, she replied to my unasked question, I did not send this woman to you, but together we all orchestrate this music. This way you got to help a woman who needed help and I got to show you something related to how I felt.

There have been a number of phases in our contact. At first, even if her thoughts came in clumps that needed translation, still they came in the realm of verbal human exchange that I can best describe as conversation. The sensation of her presence was intensely physical and easily recognized. In those early months it was almost as if we sat together over a pot of tea every morning. It all had an orderly, predictable, and relatively concrete quality. Over time that quality morphed. Her visits were more irregular; the rushing river of her energy in my body got harder to discern. We came to seem more like two people quietly reading in the same room. There was an easy sense of her love and availability, but we spoke less often and I found her words more challenging to interpret when we did. More recently the bodily tingle has become a vestige of vibration, like the kiss of a bird's breast feather falling from the sky. There are occasional bursts of profound teachings, but most of the time it resembles that comfortable sense when you know family members are at home, though you don't know exactly where they are. I wondered if this fading away was because she was moving on, or if her withdrawal was simply a reflection of my own increased balance and inner peace.

Once I came to realize that something else, with more purpose, was happening, I joked to myself that our contact was like carrying a guru in my pocket. As I recited my mantras, her presence or the lack of it became a precise gauge of the quality of my presence or the lack of it. Usually we humans are on the honor system within the privacy of our spiritual practices. Once our eyes are closed, who can tell whether we're praying or rerunning the plot of last night's movie? I have noticed that if my mind wanders, if I lose track of my place on the beads of my mala that control my count, Randi fades away, or at least my awareness of her fades. If my focus is clear and strong, so is her presence. Occasionally I lose control of the unruly horse of my mind for an entire 108 mantra set, yet I want to let it slide by as good enough. If I grab the reins and begin again, she shows her encouragement with a little extra vibration. Like an inner spiritual compass, she keeps me on course.

Early on I had asked her to tell me if she were ever visiting for the last time, so we could say our goodbyes. She replied, I will always be available to you; there will never be a last time. I envisioned an ongoing continuation of our morning chats and a growing stack of notebooks labeled "Randi Messages." Instead I am receiving lessons in recognizing her ever-more subtle presence and understanding her unspoken words. Even in her fading away, she teaches me to listen for the still, small voice within. The guru is still in my pocket, though her lessons are more challenging—like being in ADC grad school. Often I simply recognize that we will always be connected. I trust that in deep crisis she will make her presence more tangible. I also have no doubt the nature of our connection will continue to change.

Chapter Four

IS THIS A VIBRATING CHAIR?

The opposite of life is not death,
the opposite of death is birth.
Life has no opposite.
    —Found on a card with a Celtic knot printed on the back

One form of visitations that occurs while we are awake is the auditory, where we hear a voice either within ourselves or from outside. I don't always specify whether the voice was internal or external, because at first I didn't recognize the difference and so I did not think to ask. When I did start asking, people often did not know; it hadn't seemed relevant to them either. That they had heard the voice was all that counted. Auditory visitations range from times when the dead dictate entire books, through my daughter's series of brief conversations, down to single sentences or a few words like when Heidi's dead father told her, Happy birthday, daughter, just as he would have said it in life. Dorothy combined recognition of her partner's mother without the use of her five senses, followed by hearing her voice. When this woman died, her daughter, Dorothy's partner, fell apart. As Dorothy stood doing the dishes, she sensed a "presence" over her left shoulder. Then her partner's mom's voice said, very strongly, as if admonishing—I imagined a raised forefinger as I heard this—You take good care of my daughter!

⁊

Following the death of Bella's adult daughter in a car accident, Bella got reports of visitations from friend after friend after friend, though her daughter never visited her. Finally, exasperated and more than a little hurt, she demanded in a huff, "How come everyone's hearing from you except me?" The two-word response—Oh, Mom—spoke volumes. It came not only in her daughter's voice and inflection, but also in the precise words she had always used whenever she thought what her mother had said was slightly absurd. This characteristic cadence left Bella almost weak in the knees with certainty that her daughter had visited, perhaps had even been with her all along. Her daughter might as well have said, "How absurd to think otherwise, Mom." Though it's not effective for everyone, this does raise the question, could asking, even demanding, be one way to receive an after-death communication?

⁊

As Leslie described her deceased husband, she wore an expression of adoration. She said he had been a "wild child, a real rebel" with an open heart and a wicked sense of humor.

He had sailed through life way outside the mainstream, without a driver's license (though he drove) or a social security number (though he worked). He had avoided technology, even telephones ("If somebody wants to talk to me, they can come right on over."). In place of these accoutrements of modern life was an exquisite attunement with the natural world, to the falcon and to the eagle in particular. As his daughter drove to her father's remote and private burial service, she was horrified to have a falcon slam so directly into her car it seemed to her it had aimed. Fully aware of her father's affinity, she stopped to see if the falcon was all right. It had died instantly and she gently laid the limp raptor in the back of her car, handing it to her mother at the gravesite. It seemed a sacrificial symbol of Kevin's deep connection with this bird, beyond human understanding. They placed it in his grave and buried Kevin and his falcon together. Many indigenous people would call this falcon his power or totem animal, and the Maya even say that at our deaths, our power animals die too and we fly together as though we were one being into the land of the dead.[1]

Kevin may have disliked telephones, but Leslie needed a cell phone so her healing practice clients could call for appointments. The day after the burial she noted she'd not had a single phone call all day. When she checked, she found the battery uncharged, though she was positive she'd plugged the phone in the night before. She plugged it back in, surmising it must have been the grandkids. The next day, though she was alone, she found the phone unplugged and uncharged again. She wondered, was there a problem with the connection? On the third night she taped the phone to the charger. When she found it unplugged yet again in the morning, she demanded, "Okay, Kevin, are you doing this?"

Honey, you need some downtime, some quiet time for a few days, he answered. Leaving the phone off for two more days, she came to see that she did need the open-ended space of a phoneless life for a while. She still had that phone when I interviewed her seven years later, and it had never again come unplugged on its own. This experience was what Leslie needed to confirm the reality of her dead husband's continued caring presence. He was looking out for her welfare with a wisdom born of the larger view from death's treetop perch.

☙

At the time of my daughter's death I knew absolutely nothing about electrical malfunctions as communication from the dead. As we were setting up the photomontage and flowers for her memorial service, the entire windowless sanctuary went inky-black. Circuit breakers were checked and rechecked. The power had gone off, but no explanation could be found. Nothing anyone did had the least effect. Arriving guests were being held in the large, sunlit lobby, which was packed with doctors, midwives, nurses, a few mothers whose babies Randi had helped bring into life. I was astounded by how many people had come. I did not yet know this was because the women's clinic where she had worked had been closed for the morning to allow the whole staff to attend.

We lit the sanctuary with candles. Randi had adored candles, so this seemed fitting, and the space did look lovely.

Someone opened the doors. Everyone flooded in. Wes, the minister, told us afterward he had intended to ask the family how we felt about his directly addressing the issue of suicide, but in the tumult of the electrical outage, he had forgotten to ask. I was pleased when he brought this up from the pulpit, but the room stilled, with a palpable surge of energy. The clinic staff, I found out later, had not been told the cause of her death. Just as they went into shock, the lights came on bright as klieg lights. My granddaughter's father leaned close, whispering, "It's Randi!" I shot him a puzzled glance. It would be months before I understood that if Randi wanted to be sure everyone knew the cause of her death, if she wanted to emphasize how the minister's compassionate words washed suicide clean of its sinful reputation, her timing was exquisite. She had literally shed light on all this.

⁓

Synchronicity, not an uncommon component of after-death contact, is when two or more "somethings"—they could be events or objects or situations—come together in a way that conveys personal meaning. In the province of the mind, synchronicity is dismissed as mere coincidence, which does not take into account the subtle essence that empowers us to recognize a beloved (living or deceased) with something beyond our physical senses. When the dead visit us through synchronous experiences, as through electrical or physical manifestations, we can choose to honor the situation with our full attention.

Claresta and I sat on a bench on the grounds that surround the Hanuman (Hindu) Temple, where she practiced. She was in her twenties, still trying to get her bearings after the unexpected death of her not-much-older sister Theodesia. She told me of overhearing a conversation between strangers about two sisters named Claresta and Theodesia. What are the chances, with names such as theirs? Coincidence? But there is that other factor that tells Claresta, "My sister is here with me. I know it." It may seem a small thing, but to a person in grief, it can be, as it was for her, a great solace.

℘

Nora was no longer actively grieving; it had been some time since her uncle's death. She had no reason to think of him as she sat in her kitchen, alone in the house, when the four-speed fan above her range suddenly zoomed from off to maximum. "It's Uncle Glenn up to his old practical jokes," she laughed with pleasure as she so often had when he was alive. Here it is again, this instant recognition of the source of an electrical malfunction and of a beloved's essence.

The red light in the shape of a bone on Nancy's dead dog's collar—placed on her altar with other mementos of her dear departed—turned itself on every night at dusk for months. Again, Nancy knew without thought that this was a contact.

Juanita, the Mexican psychotherapist you met in chapter 2, told me of an ADC episode that occurred not long after the death of her first husband. On returning to her empty house, she was assaulted at the front door by a loud racket. Once inside, she found her empty blender running at top speed. A rational friend suggested she must surely have turned it on before she left, but she knew better. "This was Joaquin," she told me. No matter how grief-stricken, who could not hear a blender running as they locked the door and left the house?

☙

Melissa's experience takes us into the area of the manipulation, or even the temporary creation, of objects in the physical realm. This type of visitation, along with occasions like malfunctioning exhaust fans and blenders, is the source of the concept of poltergeists. Even before our interview I was taken by her description of her experience as a "tender vignette." When her mother died suddenly of a stroke at the age of eighty-two, Melissa had flown across the country and slept alone in her mother's house in the same room where she had as a child. On the morning after the funeral, as she lay awake in bed, her eyes rambled over to the hutch that had always displayed her mother's doll collection. Inside she noticed a beautiful color photograph of her mother, a recent head and shoulders shot with a quality of sheer innocence that revealed the side of her mother that had often been masked by worry. The frame was of an old-fashioned, embossed gold metal. As she lay admiring her mother, Melissa wondered why she had never seen this photo before. "This was not just a flash," she assured me. "And I was not asleep." She told me she lay, "getting my wits about me," before rising and going to the hutch to claim the photo.

To her amazement, it was not there. In fact, there were no photos or frames at all in the hutch, only dolls, as there had always been.

In that moment, Melissa knew, "She had made the journey. She had avoided any traps. She was free, dancing in delight." Since then, whenever Melissa's ordinary mind has tried to make her doubt the reality of her experience, all that has been necessary is to turn her attention to the clarity and beauty of the photo and its frame and of its effect on her to keep her doubts at bay.

❦

I relish how the dead use whatever is most conveniently at hand to let us know they are with us. Eileen's favorite aunt was in rapid decline when Eileen made one final trip cross-country to visit. On the morning of their last day together, nearsighted Eileen's glasses simply disappeared. Aunt Faye, also nearsighted, was full of concern. She made Eileen promise to let her know when she found her glasses; she would die before that would be possible. This concern and the promise set the stage for Aunt Faye to use a glasses case for contact. Back home, Eileen ordered new glasses. When she picked them up, their case was in Aunt Faye's two favorite colors— pale turquoise on one side, bright green on the other. Eileen sees and touches this case often, and each contact is a moving reminder of her aunt's love and their bond, almost as though it were a gift made by her aunt and delivered post-death. And, of course, her old glasses later surfaced in her father's car, right where she had left them.

Yuki, half-Japanese, owns a day spa here in the States. When her Great-Aunt Akiko died, the family sat together in the dining room after the service in Japan. Aunt Akiko had had the habit of offering a box of tissues around the table after a meal, repeating the English word, "Tissue? Tissue? Tissue?" to each person. A box of tissues sat on the table now and they began to wave back and forth as if in a strong wind. "It's Obasan (Grandma)," someone whispered. Someone else checked the windows and the doors. They were all tightly closed. There was no draft in the room, yet the tissues continued to wave and to wave. They all agreed this was Obasan saying goodbye. Just as the specificity of an ADC dream can align perfectly with us, it is the intimate nature of experiences like these that gives them their power to comfort. These are not just waving tissues or pretty colors. These details are the fingerprints of a personal relationship, undeniable to the people involved.

ᔥ

Now let's go back to nature and to funerals and memorial services. The dead can even conspire with something as amorphous as a cloud, shaping it into a clear message from a beloved. Most of us have looked up at recognizable white shapes silhouetted against a blue sky, yet often when I've pointed these out, focusing my finger in front of someone's eyes. "Don't you see that snout on the left? The ears? The swirl of that tail?" people have shaken their heads, pointed at a fish they could see and I could not. When the dead make the shapes, they can be so shockingly specific they rivet the attention of all those present.

Dana's daughter, Joy, had been enchanted by skulls. She had hung them on her walls; there was one on the back of her favorite hoodie, and her journals overflowed with her drawings of skulls. Dana had traveled to have a private, second memorial service with a number of Joy's friends, who had been unable to attend the first service. She made a small, clay effigy of Joy and together they buried it. As the ritual ended, everyone saw that the clouds had formed a huge and unmistakable skull, blue sky piercing its eyeholes, letting them all know Joy was with them for this ritual.

Tom saw clouds form into a perfect angel just after being told of his former mother-in-law's death. This was a woman he was fond of and who was fond of him, but they had not seen one another in twenty years. He paid little attention to the date and time of the funeral, since he knew he would not attend. A few days later, stepping outside for a breath of fresh air, he saw that the clouds had once again formed themselves into a nearly identical angel, except this time the angel's hair was wildly frizzed, which seemed to him a sign of his former mother-in-law's happiness. He felt a sudden sureness that death had somehow unburdened her. Then he remembered that it was Thursday and the precise time of the funeral, miles away. He felt she had been aware he would not be physically present and had made a special effort to include him. Here again is that reassurance that the apparent separation created by time and distance between people who care for one another is only an illusion.

When Tom's own mother died, he recalled the intensity of her concern at his father's funeral about the placement of his head up by the headstone. Back then, it had been Tom's task to remain by the grave at the service's end to ensure that placement. In honor of that concern, Tom and his niece remained by the grave at the end of his mother's service too, to confirm that her head was properly placed beside her husband's. As they waited, a hawk soared slowly by, north to south, and veered sharply to the west, where the sun sets and the direction that many indigenous peoples connect with death. The two instantly knew that this was his mother, her grandmother, telling them goodbye perhaps thanking them for performing this final, simple act of service.

Technical consultant Nadia, a diabetic, had been very much beloved by her coworkers, so when she went into insulin shock at work and died soon after, it was a blow to the entire staff. Nadia's colleague, Jeff, told me that following her memorial service, as the attendees emerged into the sunlight from her small, Canadian village church, they "were greeted by a very low-flying, indeed barely rooftop, diamond of Canada geese. More than one voice echoed, 'It was Nadia signaling us.'" Jeff called it her "fare-thee-well and all-is-well."

ↄ◌

Karen was hiking when a tiny ladybug landed on her friend's shirt and then flew to and remained inside the arm of Karen's glasses. At once she was acutely aware that this "lady" was her deceased mother. Her mom had always been reluctant to discuss family dynamics, so it was in character that, when Karen described her family as "pretty dysfunctional," the ladybug flew off. Quite soon after her father's death, Karen had another small contact through nature. The day was windless, yet a single leaf in the center of a circle of dry brown leaves on the ground began to swirl up and around. "I saw that!" she said aloud. She knew her father had made this happen, and she could feel the consolation of his company on her morning run.

❧

So far these experiences with nature have all been spontaneous, but Vivian and her doctor sister Lea were putting focus on developing their relationship with the natural world. The sisters lived half a continent apart, and for years they had practiced their esoteric capabilities by sending each other love taps through butterflies. They'd call up and say, "Thanks for the good morning," compare notes: "Yes, it was a small, yellow butterfly. Yes, it came at 10:30." They felt quite sure of themselves regarding this form of communication, so when Lea, who was much older than Vivian, was dying of cancer, Vivian knew precisely, without discussion, how Lea would visit. She would come as a small, yellow or white butterfly as she always had. Her presence would be unmistakable.

Within a few weeks of Lea's death, butterflies started coming around, closer than butterflies normally would, but they were often large and black. "Is that you, Lea?" she'd ask, but she never heard or felt a definitive reply. One after another she dismissed each butterfly as a figment of her grief and her overactive imagination. She was determined not to be satisfied with an illusion she had created for her own solace. Red-tailed hawks swooped extraordinarily near her too. Lea had volunteered at a raptor center. "Could this be my sister?" Still unsure, Vivian dismissed the hawks as well. She demanded an unequivocal sign. She would not accept anything the least bit ambiguous. One especially grief-laden night she drank a glass of wine, cried herself to sleep, and dreamed she was told Lea was in a nearby movie theater. Vivian sped on over. "Well, it is about time you showed up!" she stormed at her sister.

What do you mean? Are you kidding me? How many times did I come to you as a big, black butterfly? How many times did I have to swoop you as a red-tailed hawk?

☙

Two weeks after my daughter's death, my husband and I were returning home to New Mexico to prepare for the blessing ceremony for her soul, which our friend and spiritual counselor Cindy Lindsay had offered as a gift. I was full of trepidation. What would it be like to be in my own home knowing Randi was dead? I had clung to her home in Colorado as if by doing so I could hold the shards of our shattered family together. I fretted all the way home—about the arrangements we had made for the care of her dog and her cat, about her empty home and the possibility of thieves, about our granddaughter back in her dorm, attempting to live a normal college freshman's life.

The moment our sunporch and back door came into view we could see them. There were tens upon tens upon tens of butterflies. Yellow ones. White ones. Orange ones. Large ones. Medium ones. Tiny ones. They brushed our faces and hands and bodies as we walked the path and unlocked the door. We had to take great care or they would have come inside. They brushed us again and again as we went back and forth, unloading the car. It was impossible not to be touched by them. It was also impossible to continue my fretting, as though their wings literally lifted some of the heavy grief up and out of my body. It was late October. We live at an altitude of 7,738 feet. Our friends had harvested our pumpkins for us. The yard and flower beds were brown and dry. Hard frost had come a while back. Butterflies should have been long gone. Yet here they were, fifty of them or eighty, a hundred—who could count? They all stayed until sunset.

The next day half of them remained. I scoured the garden for flowers, finding only a few tightly closed hollyhock buds in the shelter of our *latilla* fence. A couple of the butterflies hung out one more day for the ceremony. I had laid the hollyhock buds around the bowl Cindy filled with milk, water, rose water, and a Shiva Lingam stone. Candles surrounded the bowl and the buds. Afterward, it felt wrong to blow out the candles, so I set each one in a bowl of water to let them burn out on their own time. It took two full days for the last one to go out, which seemed inordinately long. During those two days every hollyhock bud, though they lay on the cloth without water, opened and bloomed a deep, luscious red, a continuation of the ceremony to bless Randi's soul, as if nature were gently holding our hands.

I had not yet been aware of any visitations from Randi and I had never even heard of after-death communication through nature, so I hadn't stopped to ask those butterflies, "Randi, is that you?" I simply experienced their presence as a blessing. Who can resist the grace and beauty of even one butterfly, let alone fifty or a hundred? I still don't know if this blessing was "from" Randi, but it does not seem to matter to me. This was a gift from spirit, and a support when I was very much in need of gifting and support.

ඏ

My granddaughter Chelsey's last joyful memory of her mother was at her high school graduation. Four years later, in May of 2014, Chelsey completed her associate's degree in interior design, but she couldn't bring herself to participate in her graduation ceremony; it was too painful, too reminiscent of that other graduation and of her mother's death. A few weeks later as we were preparing the house Chelsey had grown up in for rental, so she could move on to complete her bachelor's, Chelsey came upon a greeting card and a folded piece of paper. Printed on the outside of the card was, "Clap! Clap! Clap! Clap!" Inside she read, "Chelsey, you graduated! Good job! Congratulations! Love, Mom" and the date: May 2004. After an incredulous pause, Chelsey explained, "It was for my sixth grade graduation!" Only one digit needed to be changed to turn 2004 into 2014.

Chelsey next unfolded the piece of paper and read aloud the poem handwritten on it. Its final lines were "We love each other, you and me, we shall love each other for eternity."

We sat side by side, alternately staring at each other in considerable confusion and rereading these words. Chelsey unfolded the paper further to a tiny picture and began to laugh through her tears.

"What? What is it?"

"It was for my hamster," she giggled. Synchronicity comes to the rescue again.

ℂℂ

Lois was a graduate student when I presented to her class on my ADC research. Her mother had died one day shy of her eighty-ninth birthday. At that time, Lois told me, she had been in the midst of a divorce and a move. She said she had no particular beliefs about an afterlife or about after-death communication, describing herself as a "wait and see" person. During the week following her mother's death Lois was disturbed several times by the strong impression of her cat padding across her bed, though the cat was not even in the room. It was her new housemate who first suggested this might be her mom visiting. It took Lois a bit of time to accept that possibility. Once she was able to, the visitations began to feel quite sweet. Then the electrical things started. The blender turned itself on in the middle of the night. Twice the television, tuned to a particular channel in the evening and turned off, was found turned on and tuned to a different channel in the morning, with a screen full of snow.

Lois had inherited her mother's favorite wingback chair and brought it into the living room of the apartment she was sharing with her friend after her divorce. This chair was where she sat in the evenings with her cat purring in her lap, where she read or talked or watched television. On the first Christmas morning following her mother's death, a guest Lois barely knew, her housemate's friend, chose to sit in that wingback chair. A moment later she leapt up with a bewildered expression on her face, demanding, "Is this a vibrating chair?"

"No. It's not. It was my mother's. It's just a regular chair." The woman cautiously sat back down. In only a moment she leapt up again and moved across the room to another seat, glancing periodically at the wingback chair as if it were possessed. Think about what an empty chair represents. It is an invitation that offers support. This upholstered one added the soft comfort and arms and wings of an embrace filled with maternal energy. On this Christmas morning, her mother made it clear these gifts were only for Lois, not for just any old near-stranger.

What is it about these simple events that gives them such personal significance? How is it that we can recognize the presence of someone we love with such certainty, when we humans are so accustomed to communicating through words? To recognize their presence we don't attend to them in our usual way. Perhaps it is an old way we have nearly forgotten, like what the Japanese samurai called the *kan*, where we look beneath the surface of a thing into its essence. Because of our heart connection with our dead beloveds, love carves out an opening through which they can soar in a form we can recognize.

There is no need to explain anything, nothing to figure out or to prove; we only need to attend to the birds, to the butterflies, and even to the malfunctions of our blenders and exhaust fans. The dead do seem fond of things that make a lot of noise. In some inexplicable manner, all things and beings seem capable of being in cahoots with our dead beloveds, who are eager to contact us however they can. These diverse visitations may not appear on the surface to have much in common—a phone that won't stay plugged in, a disappearing photo, a hundred out-of-season butterflies— yet at their core such experiences lift grief's burden enough so we can go on, while moving us inexorably closer to awareness of life's continuity.

Chapter Five

JUST CHECKING IN

Grace is not something you can demand.
You can only sweep out the chamber of your soul and
be ready to receive it when it comes.
—**Mirabai Starr, God of Love**

Death is a shadow that haunts us from that first moment in childhood when we understand that whoever it is, Grandma perhaps, or Great-Aunt Millie, is not going to be coming home next week, or the week after either. Where has she gone? And will I go, too? And will Mum? And what can I do to stop this going away and never, ever coming back? I had always assumed this fear of death was universal, until I came upon Vine Deloria Jr. writing that members of tribal cultures who don't consider death as a foe to be vanquished are not so afraid of death.[1] Nevertheless, most people in modern culture do not fully recover from these fears upon reaching adulthood, so it is a blessing that death is often surrounded by a compassionate force I call grace that brings an extra dollop of support. Sometimes this grace comes to the one who is dying, sometimes to the ones who will live. It can precede the death, giving us a tiny bit of preparation. It can come at the moment of death, informing us of a death when we are not at the deathbed or uplifting us if we are. It can follow the death swiftly or wait some considerable amount of time before coming.

Grace warns us, gives us an arm to lean on to help us work through our terrors and our sorrow. A woman who shared stories of an exceptional number of losses described this force as cocooning her, as though she were enfolded in the soft comfort of cotton wool, a gentle presence surrounding her heart and mind to keep the illusion of death from making too great a wound, until she "could process the event." My friend Jillis says this grace is death "flipping the windows open," so we know what we would not ordinarily know, make decisions against all logic, choose the perfect words to heal an old wound without being aware that it is our last opportunity to do so.

෫ා

At four o'clock one morning Celeste and her husband were awakened by a crash so loud they both jumped from bed, checked the house, checked the yard. Finding nothing amiss, they returned to bed. In a few minutes the phone rang. Her husband said, because his father had been ill, "It's my father."

"No," Celeste countered, "it's *my* father." While her husband answered the phone, her father appeared to her in a vision at the foot of the bed. The phone call was to notify them of his death from a heart attack. Being directly informed in such a visual manner, close to the moment of death, penetrates our bodies and our psyches with a less shocking and more compassionate tone than the most caring phone call ever could. A call gives us facts, but the direct contact communicates that the loving connection with this person has not ceased. No words were spoken, but Celeste also knew her father was all right. Reflecting back on foreknowledge like that strange crash can slide the death a little bit sideways into another perspective and ease its blow.

∞

Heidi's parents were experiencing the health issues that may accompany the end of long lives. Her mother was living with Alzheimer's in a nursing home, but it was her father who died first. That summer, Heidi had tucked a tiny glass bluebird into the corner of his coffin. The following February, as her mother's death approached, Heidi had a painfully unsatisfying dream in which her mother was naked and the "purest of whites," at the bottom of a huge hole. She needed help, but she could not receive it from Heidi. This dream recurred the next night with a significant change: now a helper sat inside the hole beside her mother. In both dreams her mom glowed a transcendent white. As though they were one, the two dreams transmitted the reassurance that her mother was getting the help she needed as she prepared to die.

February is still deep winter where Heidi lives in Pennsylvania; there was snow on the ground. At her mother's bedside, Heidi prayed, "Dad, I hope you are around to help

Mom." Out of the corner of her eye she glimpsed the impossible: on a leafless tree a bluebird frantically hopped up and down. She turned to look at it head-on. Impossible or not, this was a bluebird. The instant she acknowledged this as fact, the bird stood still, peering in at her as if it were her father saying, I'm here. Don't worry. I'm waiting.

One morning she awakened at 2:22, knowing, before the phone rang, that her mother had died. Twenty minutes later, she found her mother's face surrounded by tiny, sparkling lights. Heidi's experiences encompassed five types of ADC, if we include the synchronicity that now, whenever she notices that the clock reads 2:22, it signals awareness of her mother's presence.

℘

Emily is the woman in chapter 2, a fantastic professional baker, who delivered a dream message to someone she barely knew. On this particular occasion she had been unreachable by telephone for several days. Early on Sunday morning she dreamed a "stunningly beautiful young man aglow with a heavenly light" stood facing her. I love you and I hope this helps, he said, handing her a box. She awoke bathed in this man's love for her. On her return home, she received a call from her mother telling her that her father had died at six o'clock on Sunday morning. At once Emily knew who the beautiful young man in her dream had been. She could only recall one other time when her father had said, "I love you," so this dream's impact was enormous. Because of the delay in receiving the call, and because her mother, who was showing early signs of Alzheimer's, gave her inaccurate information, Emily did not make it to her father's service. She believes he visited her so forcefully because he knew this would occur. The box turned out not to be symbolic, for he had willed her a box of valuable coins that helped her through a low spot in her finances.

Now Emily's former partner has been hospitalized. She cannot visit him, because his family is with him and blames her for leaving him when he was ill, though she had not known. In fact, she had urged him to see a doctor, but he had told her, "I would rather die." Now he is dying. At 3:30 on this afternoon, as Emily meditates and prays for him, she sees a brilliant light and feels an overwhelming sense of peace. Wondering if he has just died, she opens her journal to write what she will say at his memorial service. He does die that day, though she is told this occurs hours later. At the service she reads what she has written, mentioning the 3:30 time. Afterward his niece, moved to connect by Emily's story and tears, tells her he had actually died at 3:30, explaining that, as they awaited the arrival of one last relative, the breathing machine was kept connected; the official time of death, which was what Emily had been given, was not recorded until after this machine was disconnected.

ঙ৩

Kent had been an athlete and was still a vigorous man when he was diagnosed with metastasized melanoma. After six challenging months, he told his wife, Mimi, "Tomorrow's the day." When tomorrow arrived, as Mimi lay beside him, he asked her if she was going to be all right. She told him that she was devastated but that she would be all right. "Good," he replied. Good was to be his last word while still alive.

Like a dancer, Mimi gracefully gathered her cupped hands in front of her abdomen as she told me how it felt as Kent was dying and his spirit moved through her body. "It was as though I levitated. I lifted right off the bed." She drew her hands slowly up the front of her torso. "Whooosh— he was gone." Her hands shot above her head. The tension and strength in Mimi's long fingers conveyed as much as she could of the visceral quality and strength of this visitation; her words were nearly superfluous. She repeated, with more emphasis, "He was gone, just gone."

Mimi called Kent's friends in from the other room. For thirty more minutes he breathed what is known as the agonal breath, though the agony may be more for the living than for those who are dying, who have often, as Kent had done, already vacated their bodies. Everyone gathered around him, touching him, singing "Amazing Grace," Mimi told me. "This was one of the most powerful events of my life. It taught me about love, about letting go, about grace."

Kent has visited her many times since in dreams. Once— not in a dream—she saw him sitting in the chair where he had received his morphine. As she drove, a little too fast on a snowy road, she felt his hand come to rest on top of hers on the gearshift and his voice say, Slow down. Moments like this allow the tender threads of a partnership to dissolve slowly, long after the initial numbing shock of the physical death. Grief and loss weaken us at first. Their burden is so heavy it can crush us, especially if we believe our beloveds have simply ceased to be.

☙

Molly was unaware of a reason to grieve when the disabling difficulty began in her shoulder. It became immobilized overnight, too painful even to be touched. This meant she was completely unable to do her work as a physical therapist. No known cause for this pain could be ascertained. No healing modality had the least effect. On a skilled hunch her psychotherapist friend asked, "What does this pain remind you of?"

Molly looked inward, and much to her own surprise, whispered, "My brother's death." Her brother had drowned decades earlier at age five, when Molly had been only two years old.

"And what does this pain look like?"

"A huge dragon."

An entire week was spent at home, in what Molly describes as an altered state, looking this dragon in its fiery face. As a child Molly had been encouraged only to forget, not to grieve, the loss of her big brother. Now, as she worked through this long-buried emotional pain, her shoulder torment shrank from huge dragon to tiny lizard. It was grace that on Sunday of that same week, when her teenaged stepson was killed in a car accident, she was available in a way she is convinced she would not have been a week earlier for both her own sorrow and that of her husband and their other children. She told me, "Without switching gears, I could move into the new grief." As she said this, tears of gratitude welled in her eyes for "this presence, this force," as she called it. That dragon had been barricaded so deeply in the grief point of her heart, and for such a long time, that grace had to ramrod the door open in order to release it.

Many of us have grief from old losses stashed within us, because the generations before us often knew no other way to deal with emotional pain than to deny it, so we have learned from wounded teachers. Yet if we close over grief without expressing or processing it, it's like sewing closed a surgical wound with the infection still inside; the scar may look benign, but the infection is likely to surface sooner or later.

౪

Valerie is an adventurous bird-lover from the United States who abandoned the corporate life to travel extensively throughout Latin America. Now she has settled in Oaxaca, Mexico, where we spoke. She told me that as she traveled she had kept up erratic connections with friends and family whenever she could get online, often racing through her e-mails at warp speed at the end of a long day. One afternoon at an Internet café in Argentina, she had been thrilled to see her friend Rod's name appear in her inbox. Rod had been her inspiration for going on this journey, following his lead to go where her heart called. As long as she had known him, he had gone through periodic bouts with skin cancer, so when he had e-mailed her about some more, she had thought little of it. He seemed to her unstoppable, forever having growths removed, undergoing treatment, continuing on. He hadn't answered her most recent e-mails, and she missed him. This one, however, was not from Rod but from his daughter, informing her of his death. Reeling in shock and confusion, she dove back into their old e-mails looking for clues. Guilt raised its horned head once she realized how she had glossed through them, only focusing on how each e-mail had ended: "but I'm okay." As she carefully reread every word, she saw just how many treatments he had mentioned. She was horrified to find one reference to Stage IV cancer. How had she missed that?

"Why wasn't I there for him? Why did I let him down?" Wrapped in grief and self-censure, she trudged back to her tiny, rented house. There on the sidewalk between her landlord's house and hers were two of her favorite fat, strutting birds with little tufted-feather topknots. She had seen them in Colombia. She had seen them in Panama. What were they doing here in Argentina as winter was about to set in? It was the wrong season for these funny birds whose name she could no longer recall as we spoke. Her eyes were drawn to the roof. Perched on its peak were three small birds of prey—kestrels she thought. "He's okay," washed through her. And again, "Rod is okay." The birds, it seemed to her, announced this. Her grief remained, but the great weight of guilt lifted. She was fully convinced that Rod, aware of her affinity for birds, had sent them to comfort and relieve her, to separate her grief from her guilt. The dead appear to know precisely what we need and just as precisely how we can best receive it.

⌘

Kerry was in her thirties when her fifty-one-year-old husband was hospitalized to undergo an angioplasty the next morning. She had left overnight to be with their five-year-old daughter and dreamed she and her daughter were joined together into one being. They climbed high up into the sky and back down again on an exquisite silver cord. This exhilarating climb granted her a glimpse of a reality much vaster than our mortal life. She awoke with a jerk, as though returning to her body. Meanwhile her sister, without telling Kerry and acting on pure instinct or, as I call it, a strong nudge from grace, had spontaneously driven nine hours to be with her. Because of this nudge, the sisters were together as Kerry was told her husband had not survived this "routine" surgery.

ᏕᎱ

Sarah's mother lived in a nursing home following a series of ministrokes. Sarah lived a distance away and visited when she could. Money was tight; no current trip was planned. One of her brothers had recently gone to see their mother and noticed nothing out of the ordinary, but suddenly Sarah knew that, tight money or not, she must go right away. On arrival she saw instantly that her mother was dying. She had to convince her three brothers to come. "But I just saw her. She's fine," the one argued. As the brothers were arriving, her mother asked Sarah, "Are all the boys here?" Two were, one was still traveling. Sarah answered yes, as we might to a child, to ease her mother's concerns. "No, they're not," her mother replied. The dying may be harder to mollify than the rest of us. Her mother died with Sarah's hand on her heart and each of her three sons touching her.

∾

The quiet call of death can be difficult to recognize. Sadness flecked with regret flared in Nicole's eyes as she told me of her dream before her father's death years earlier. She had dreamed of her parents' bedroom in her childhood home. Because the pole on which they had once hung their clothes held only her mother's clothing, Nicole awoke certain her father would die in the near future. She and the man who was then her partner were preparing to leave for France. She wanted to change their plans, delay their trip; she allowed him to convince her otherwise. Once they arrived in France, Nicole knew her father was dead by the expression on the face of their friend who met the plane. Learning to listen to and interpret the inner guidance we receive is one of life's more exacting tasks. Nicole's dream was clear and she had read it correctly, but it did not tell her in which part of the "near future" her father would die.

Thea shared a dream that foretold of her husband's death, where she could see her own face in the bathroom mirror but could not see his, though he stood behind her. Like Nicole, she knew this meant her husband would die, but when? How soon? His health began to fail soon after, but he lived another year. This could well have been the case for Nicole's father. How can we know?

As he lay beside his wife, Terry saw a light in their bedroom that was visible even with closed eyes. When he realized it was a woman he had dated years earlier, it seemed to him an invasion of their marital space to have an old girlfriend in the bedroom. He turned away; the light left. He later discovered this woman had recently died. Why would she have come to him when he did not view their connection as particularly strong? He too showed a smidgeon of regret as he told me he wondered what might have happened had he been more welcoming.

We don't learn everything on the first try. We gain as much, often more, from a choice that leaves us with regrets as we do from a choice that pleases us. Over time we come to interpret our dreams and nudges in a way that can soften and ease the events of our lives. If Nicole has another dream that presages a death, she will attend to her inner knowing differently. And Terry is less likely to turn away from a strange light in his bedroom.

ℰℐ

Lynnette's grace story is a satisfying one despite the fact that her mother was ill for four years before dying when Lynnette was only sixteen. It illustrates how it is possible for a dying mother to pass on a positive effect to her daughter. This effect still manifests in Lynnette's mature voice as a soft serenity. I heard sadness, but I did not hear pain. She told me that because her mother had been so open and direct, "We were able to say all we needed to say." Even at sixteen she knew they left behind no unfinished business. She was "the nicest mother I knew," Lynnette said. During the final hospitalization, as her mother lay in a coma, Lynnette said to her, "We (the family) are going to be okay." What made this so satisfying was Lynnette's awareness that her mother had heard her words.

A few days post-death, Lynnette dreamed her mother came to reassure her one more time. I'm fine, she said. I'm okay. I will always be with you. By the clarity and honesty of her communication, Lynnette's mother reduced the shock of trauma both before and after her death, so that Lynnette was not overwhelmed by grief.

ↄ

Three vibrant points of grace surrounded my parents' deaths in 1984. My mother had been brought home to die. "Three Months to a Year" flashed like a neon sign in the air above the bed. I drove the two-hundred-mile round-trip every week to be there for the aide's days off. On this day, I had left my parents' house for a midday walk, and I was whining about how my mother was going to die "on me" without us ever having even one significant conversation. I had worked myself up into quite a state of self-pity when the very distinct voice of what sounded like a caricature of a mother in a Woody Allen film interrupted my snivel. So who's holding a gun to your head? the voice said. I could almost see the lifted hands, the shrugged shoulders. You wanna talk, talk. I skidded to a stop, turned to my right. No one was there. To my left. No one. I looked *up*. Of course, no one was in the sky either. I turned in a full circle. Suddenly feeling ridiculously conspicuous, I walked on, pondering. Regardless of where this voice came from, whoever this woman was, she was wise and she was right. *I* was the one with something to say, and *I* had full control over my side of any conversation I might have with my mother. I hustled my father off to his afternoon at the office with a kiss and asked her, "Do you still want me to file your nails?" It was two o'clock as I placed her hand in mine. I gulped and took a long, full breath and sank the sword to its hilt. "It's not so much the drinking that was the problem, Mother, as the lying about it."

Here the terrain got strange. The next memory I have is of wondering why the light was so dim and discovering it was five o'clock. We had been engrossed in conversation for three full hours, though I could not recall one word beyond my initial sentence. Decades of silence and strain had disintegrated. I felt lighthearted and free; my mother looked softer, younger. She kept smiling. I could only surmise that what we said was not the point, that our words must have bypassed our minds, gone straight from heart to heart. My mother's alcoholism could not be undone, yet our relationship shifted on its axis that afternoon. Did I forgive her? Did she apologize? I only know that something broken was mended, something was all right between us that had not been, and all because of that disembodied voice. Why the New York accent? Just to get my attention? Or to show me that grace has a sense of humor? Because I needed to lighten up? Or because the voice was so distinctly neither mine nor my family's, I could not possibly hear it as my own mind's chatter?

We had arranged that when "she's going to die" advanced to "she's dying," my sister and I would both come and stay for the duration. This advance only took a few weeks. I arrived home one evening to a machine full of progressively more panicked messages from my father that each began with, "She says it's time!" I packed my bags to cross the Delaware River from Pennsylvania into New Jersey in the morning. I scanned my bookshelves for something to read aloud that might please and uplift us both. Where was that Dorothy Bryant visionary novel, *The Kin of Ata Are Waiting for You,* that begins with a murder by a hard-drinking, hard-drugging man, then transmogrifies into a transcendent tale of spirit in which he sheds his addictions?[2] Oh—I suddenly recalled I'd loaned it to my friend Jillis; I would swing by for it on my way out of town. But in the morning Jillis had gone out for an hour and neither her husband nor I could find the book. I waited. Jillis was late. Still, I waited. I did not yet know that it was grace that had me fixated on reading this particular book—no other would do—to my dying mother.

My sister Eve and I took turns reading aloud. Our mother lay so still, we couldn't tell if she was listening until we came to a slower-paced page or two, when she snapped, "Get on with it already." An absurd pang of hope flared within me and as quickly died out; one revival of her old literary sensibilities did not mean my mother would survive this cancer. We didn't know what she thought when we read about painkillers and about addiction. She had not been on an alcohol binge for the year of her illness, though now, on a regular schedule, our father gave her shots of prescribed medication for bone cancer pain. We had been told this pain could be severe, yet she never complained and we never saw the slightest evidence of it. Eve and I whispered out of earshot upstairs, "Is this just another way to feed her addiction?" We worried. And we read on. The stale smell of illness was alive in the dining room where the rented hospital bed had replaced the round oak table. Sometimes we quietly cried as we read about the kin of Ata who live, guided by their dreams, on a tiny island with limited cultivation space and very little food. One of the kin has dreamed that the way to survive is to feed one another, never to feed themselves, so all food is given as a gift and is therefore more nourishing. Mother had stopped eating. She had not said more than five words in as many days.

On this day our father came home from the office at noon. As the back door opened, Mother's eyes did, too. She mumbled something. "What?" We leaned close. "Apple?" we deciphered after numerous guesses. "You want an apple?" She nodded. We were incredulous. She has not eaten in a week and now she wants an apple? I washed an apple, polished it until the red shone. It seemed vital that this fruit be beautiful. Her eyes flew open again. "Apple. Ray." Ray, our father, sat in his wheeled office chair beside her bed.

A sliver of the significance of what was about to happen became clear to me and my sister simultaneously. Jean, the aide, intuitive as always, disappeared upstairs, though we didn't notice her absence until afterward. "What's going on?" Daddy frowned. We didn't know what to explain. "Wait, wait. You'll see," one of us replied. My sister sliced the apple paper-thin. I washed a crystal plate. It felt as though we were following instructions.

"What's happening?" Daddy grumbled, looking baffled. Mother looked asleep, though we knew she wasn't. Eve sensed that even a slender slice would be too much for Mother to eat. She minced one into tiny fragments. We arrayed the cut apple in a delicate mandala and placed the plate on the bed by her frail hand.

"Mother, here it is. Here's the apple."

"What's this all about?"

"Shhh, just wait. You'll see." Our mother held a slice toward our father's mouth. Her hand shook; her eyes were alert now and shining, focused on his.

"Daddy, eat the apple."

"But . . ."

"We'll explain later. Please, just eat it. Please." He did. Now his eyes too were locked on hers. Mother gave a firm and satisfied nod, her sallow face suddenly lit from within. She signaled from the plate to her beloved to her mouth. He frowned again, darting his eyes back to us. "Feed her a tiny piece."

"But she's not eating."

"Right now she is. Feed her." He did.

This was a sacrament as holy as that in any church or temple or mosque. She fed him. He fed her. The room was alive with the history of their nearly half a century of loving. Though they each had spoken to us about the reality that she was dying, they had been unable to speak of this with one another. Whatever it was that had constricted their words no longer mattered. This was the rich, red glow of the sunset before night falls into darkness. This was my mother thanking my father for the life they had shared, nourishing him with her love and him nourishing her in return. Even in his confusion, color flooded his grieving face. Something beatific bathed them both.

Surely this spontaneous ceremony emerged from more than a novel and our mother's response to it. This scene rings in me still like a bell that annihilates all the labels and terms that could apply to my family: alcoholic, co-dependent, dysfunctional. The words crumble and dissolve and whisper, just as the dead so often do: It's all okay. Nothing is a mistake.

In the kitchen, later, we tried to explain to our father as much as we understood at that moment. We read him relevant passages from the book. His mind still couldn't quite grasp the meaning, yet his eyes reflected that he too felt the grace. Suddenly he recalled he had forgotten her noontime pain shot and hurriedly returned to the dining room. As he gave her the shot, grace offered me and Eve the next shift, which, a few minutes later, as Mother rested, caused us to tell him, "We don't think she'll need any more shots."

"But what about her pain? The cancer? The nurse said to always . . ."

"We know. We don't want her to hurt. If she asks for a shot, give it to her, but we don't think she will." Our mother never again asked for or received pain medication of any kind. It would be a few more sweet, sweet days before she shrank inward into full silence. The last two weeks of our addictive mother's life were lived pain-free and substance-free.

The ancient Greek poet Pindar said that the "Three Graces" of mythology were created to fill the world with pleasant moments and goodwill. Two of my three graces were the conversation with my mother and the sacrament of the apple. There had already been a third grace, a month or so earlier, though its full meaning was not yet revealed. Once we had known that my mother would die, my father had asked me and my husband to move into the house to care for her, and I had balked. My mother's illness had exhausted me already. I was newly remarried, and although my husband was willing to move with me, I foresaw his casual ways and my parents' stringent ones exploding into fireworks. I'm not sure my husband quite believed me when I described how carefully my father washed his change whenever he emptied his pockets. My husband had no idea of the maelstrom that would erupt if he were seen picking up a dropped dish towel and continuing to use it. This household had a very specific code of behavior, and still, at that point, there were tremendous tensions among us. Two days a week with my parents gave me five in which to recover.

I spent the days before my next visit agonizing over how to turn down my father's so reasonable request. Any loving daughter would say yes, but would I, or my marriage, survive such a year? Like a memory from the future I foresaw how my father would respond to my refusal: "She is your mother. We don't want some stranger to live in our house." Some stranger who might stumble upon the secrets, unearth a few hidden vodka bottles, I wondered? When I arrived, I settled on the piano bench, my back ramrod straight. My father sat in his usual place on the couch. Anxiety filled the living room. My hands were sweaty. "I'm afraid," I gulped. "I'm afraid you'll think I don't love you when I say no."

"Do you?" he squeaked out, his voice nearly swallowed by his failed attempt to hold back tears. I was astonished. I had never seen my father cry. Had he even heard that I had said no?

"I do love you, very, very much." Then I was crying, too, the depth of our habitual constraint suddenly unmasked. We had been led to this moment and to the emotional conversation that followed. Afterward there was a gentle ease between us. Once my mother and I had our talk, peace settled among the three of us. Some of the family's corners had been swept clean. The spiderwebs were gone, the dust, there were no longer so many greasy fingerprints on the windows. I did not know that day that my father would die barely two weeks after my mother, yet in the midst of my suffering those "Three Graces" accomplished their aim; they brought goodwill and pleasant moments. And in the end, the whole family benefited from the grounded, caring, experienced presence of Jean, the woman we hired to help us.

From these grace experiences has come a profound respect for the possibilities inherent in the dying process. I consider the year of my mother's cancer to be her final great gift, the one that cauterized her many acts of commission and omission. That moment of sacramental ceremony stripped my parents to the essence of their love. In the last weeks of her life, my mother's dying restored our family to its highest potential.

⚬

Hal's episode of grace stands at the threshold of the totality of what most of us are capable of fathoming about consciousness. He is the man in chapter 2 whose decade of dreams after the death of his young friend Donnie had awakened him to the ineffable. Hal had told me of yet another early experience in the realms of mystery. As a young man he had had emergency surgery for a burst brain embolism. In the middle of the night he lay awake in his darkened room in great pain and close to death. The door opened. Hal's tiny grandmother, his mother's mother, was silhouetted against the hospital hallway's bright light. She entered, carrying a stack of dinner plates, which she distributed, one by one, on every available surface. He scrutinized her every move, especially aware of the loud sound each plate made as it was clanked down. She left the way she had entered, without speaking or acknowledging him. In the morning, Hal's mother called from her hotel across the street in an agitated state. She too had been awake in the night, so convinced her mother was in the hotel, she had gotten up to let her in but, "When I opened the door, the hall was empty."

"I think you need to get right over here. I have something to tell you." Hal replied. This could be only another startling ADC story, but it contains an element beyond that of accepting that the dead can visit us because, though living at a distance and definitely not in the hospital physically, Hal's grandmother was very much alive. In that day's mail, he received a card from her with a picture of a tiny, grandmotherly woman peeking around a slightly ajar door. The card read, "Just checking in." Hal began to heal that day. Of course he asked himself, how could his grandmother have come in this way? And even if he wondered if he had hallucinated, there was also his mother's certainty that his grandmother had been across the street. Why the plates? Did they represent the meals still to come in his life or the ones his grandmother would serve him? Had she helped him to heal somehow, perhaps even saved his life?

Grace can have so many names, be described in so many ways. It comes in whatever form and manner will be effective, with neither boundaries nor limitations. It sees a need, seeks an opening, and presents itself. Whether it comes with the protection of a cocoon or with a New York accent, it takes whatever shape gets us to notice and to listen. It is an opened window, a breath of fresh air in a stifling room. We fill our lungs and breathe easier, cleansed and strengthened to face the next moment. It is by this strengthening, and by the sudden shift, that we recognize its presence.

Chapter Six

IS THERE A SHADOW SIDE?

*From ghoulies and ghosties and long-leggety beasties
And things that go bump in the night, Good Lord,
deliver us!*

—**Cornish prayer**

Initially I had no intention of focusing on the shadow side of after-death communication. After all, we don't need deliverance from those malfunctioning blenders and alarm systems that go bump in the night. Our world seems already way too attentive to the bothersome ghosts and zombies and poltergeists that the media magnify out of all proportion. The fear engendered by this treatment only adds to our fear of the unknown and interferes with, or even distorts, loving contacts into something frightening. I was asked about the shadow side often enough to recognize the need to examine the occasional, isolated incident. What I found was that frightening experiences are opportunities to develop our own strengths. Those without bodies have no more power over us than we grant them, and we grant them power through fear. Our strongest ally is to reject any contact that is less than comfortable, anything potentially disturbing, regardless of its source, while simultaneously responding with the utmost compassion for the dead. Where the shadow side enters the picture is with some—not all—of those dead who have been unable to cross fully over into death for a variety of reasons I will discuss. Rest assured, dark experiences are rare with our beloveds.

Disturbing contacts may come from someone we don't know who is attached to a location, or we may have contact (again, only occasionally) with a beloved who, via addiction, suicide, murder, or some other violent or sudden death, has not fully crossed over. In an ideal world, all the dead would be supported to complete the process by people expert in such work, but even among those who have not crossed over directly, most contacts are benign with no intent to harm. I'll begin with several classic haunted-house situations.

ↄ

The one time I had contact where I could actually see the dead was on February 1, 1985. I recall the date, because it was the day my husband and I had rented and moved into a large Victorian house, originally built as a summer home, half a block from the Atlantic Ocean. Though a furnace had been installed, it was still typically used as a summer and weekend retreat and, for all I know, may never before have been occupied full-time in February.

My husband had gone away overnight. I thought I was alone in the house. It was late evening. I was unpacking cutlery and dishes, surrounded by crumpled newspaper and boxes, when I got the unsettling sensation of eyes boring into the back of my head. I leapt up and wheeled around, peering through the unlit living room. On the landing stood a tall, slender woman, her dark hair pulled back severely. She wore a bustled, maroon velvet Victorian dress with white lace trim. The expression on her face must have mirrored my own. "Who the hell are you?" it demanded. "And what the hell are you doing in *my* home?" We stared at one another for a timeless moment, and then slowly, rather like the Cheshire Cat, she faded away before my eyes. I did no more unpacking that night. To get upstairs to the bedroom I had to cross that landing, and, in case you're wondering, no, there was no cold spot where the woman had stood. Our bedroom had two doors. Only one would lock and I locked it, laughing at myself as I did so. What good was one locked door? And did I really imagine that even two could keep out this uninvited guest?

I slept restlessly and felt relieved when my husband returned the next day. Together we made a plan in case this woman came back—which she did with a vengeance. For hours over each of the next two nights we heard a wild banging in the attic, as though someone were dragging a string of tin cans back and forth over the rafters. My husband sat up on the couch downstairs; I sat up in bed; and we each talked ourselves hoarse to this ghostly woman. I made it up as I went along, things like, "You may not know it, but you have died. We imagine this must have been your home. But now you have a new home, and it's best that you go to it.

You will find those you love there and helpers and teachers. Being in this house does not serve you anymore." I talked as I would to any lost and unhappy person. I don't know what my husband told her, but late on our second mostly sleepless night the banging stopped. The difference in the house was tangible. In the eight months we lived there, we never again felt her presence.

౿

Lauren bought and moved into an old farmhouse that had been owned by an elderly woman, whose drug-addicted sons had inherited it, neglected it, and abused it before Lauren and her partner purchased it. They scrubbed and cleaned, stripped wallpaper, painted. Periodically, a smell Lauren described with a grimace as "a stale, old-lady perfume" wafted from an upstairs closet. (This is the same Lauren whose dead father announced himself with the smell of liverwurst and A&D Ointment.) Lauren and her partner could both smell this perfume, and they wondered if it was connected to the former owner. No amount of cleaning or airing or painting this closet made the least difference; the smell came and went when it pleased. One day, a tiny slip of paper fluttered down from a high shelf downstairs; on it was the former owner's obituary. Armed now with a name, the next time the perfume arrived, Lauren entered the closet, sat down, and gently told the woman they had bought the house because they loved it and she need not feel concern for it any longer. The smell of perfume never returned again. There was no need to mention that the woman was dead or to refer to spirit. Here was someone who must have cared for her home very much. Lauren's reassuring words were all that was required.

Rita, too, lived in an old farmhouse her husband had long ago inherited from his father. Rita said it had "scared the bejesus" out of her when she saw a shadow move from her dead father-in-law's former bedroom and on out the kitchen door. The second time she saw this shadow, she was sure it was her father-in-law, so she formed a mental picture of him going away and told him, "It's time for you to leave. It's time for you to move on. This is our house now." He too never came again. In these cases, we can only hope that the dead were released from their unhealthy ties to the earth plane. Without the expert's ability to ascertain the state of their souls, we only know they've left us alone. This may be the most we can do by ourselves.

&

When addictive people die, they may so crave their substance of choice that they seek out a living body through which to imbibe. An alcoholic woman, before she quit drinking, once saw many hideous entities in a bar, hovering above the heads of the patrons awaiting their next drinks. (Is it any wonder she quit?) Another woman saw an ugly entity emerging from her dying alcoholic father and "eyeing her up" as if she would be next. Using her well-developed spiritual skills, she turned to her inner guide and offered her father to Spirit for healing, passing along the attached entity in the process.

In the following experience, my interviewee Valerie attended a man's memorial service with her former partner, who was this man's friend. There is much that is unknown, since the man's family excluded his friends from their lives soon after his death. After being asked to leave the family business due to drinking issues, he had hung himself on the premises. Two memorial services were to be held, one in the room where he had hung himself and the other across the country where he had once lived. Both services were delayed, one by a tornado watch, the other by a fire. The sum total of these details, including that the family made the ghoulish choice to leave the hanging rope up in full sight during the first service, strongly suggests considerable dysfunction. Experiences through the veil reveal a continuity that does not allow for avoidance of family issues. Whatever the wound or the trouble, it remains, still in need of healing and resolution; it asks to be addressed, not denied. I sense this situation could have been eased by expert support to release the dead man's soul, along with someone to help the family on this side of the veil with their interpersonal issues.

I have no idea if the dead man caused the tornado watch and the fire, although I can't rule this out as impossible. What I am reminded of is how Randi had used the incident I have already described, when I helped a woman in the midst of a panic attack, to illustrate how frightened Randi herself had felt before her death. She told me this kind of confluence of events is how the world works; the woman received help, and my understanding of Randi's condition was deepened. The fire, the tornado watch, the hanging rope seem to be such a confluence, although the opportunity to use this for healing or understanding may not have been taken.

Some upsetting contacts may only be indications of a misplaced desire for control by the dead. Kerry's life was secure after her husband's death. She had a young child, but she owned her home outright and her work was solid and well-paid. Seven years later, ready to take some risks, she sold the house and resigned her position to move to a new locale. Her husband told her in a dream, angry and full of judgment, You're throwing away all I worked so hard for. This dream troubled her, but she went forward with her plans. Perhaps, even as a dead parent, he still felt some level of responsibility for his child. Yet I notice that, though he expressed his view strongly, he waited to do so until *after* she had sold the house and left her job, when it would have been difficult to change plans. Perhaps he was both acknowledging her right to take risks and reminding her to take the same good care of their child that he would have, had he lived.

෴

Celeste describes her first husband, who died by suicide, as the "love of my life." His head—just his head—had been seen and photographed under her chair at a séance soon after his death, though the photo was withheld from her for years as too frightening. He came as a head with no body to their children, who had not found this frightening. Celeste went on to have other relationships with men, but she always held some part of herself in abeyance. On this night, in bed with a lover, she noticed a little sparkle of light across the room.

It moved closer and transformed into the head of her dead husband, who told her to go with love, just as she climaxed. This contact helped her to release the last vestiges of her "survivor's guilt." After she told her friends of her experience, they finally showed her the séance photo. She is convinced that had she known he was with her so early on, it would have been easier to release her guilt more quickly. Even the disembodied head of one's beloved still carries his or her dear face and need not be a cause for fear.

☙

Vivian's husband was driving as they traveled to join the rest of his family after her brother-in-law's death from illness at age thirty-six. He appeared to Vivian in her mind. She could see him clearly and feel his presence all around her. I'm going to show you something, he said. You have to tell everyone.

"I don't want to do that. Why don't you just go to them directly?"

They can't see me. You have to tell them.

"I don't want to."

You have to or I'll haunt you.

"Okay, I'll tell the first person. If they don't think I'm nuts, I'll tell the next, but you cannot haunt me!" He showed himself to her at about eighteen, wearing a bright orange-printed shirt with mother-of-pearl snaps. Vivian described this to her husband.

"I know that shirt," he shot back.

"Oh, no, now I have to tell the next one," she grumbled to herself. This shirt seemed a kind of talisman, because when she did tell the next person, he recalled it, too. So it went, until she had described this shirt to every family member. They each had a clear memory of that particular article of clothing. Of course, this was a grace experience, because they were each relieved to know his essence was still "alive" and well, but why did he threaten to haunt Vivian? What is key to note is how Vivian handled his threat: she simply refused to allow him to haunt her. Their negotiation was only about what he was asking of her. On the haunting she stood firm. And I note that he was newly dead.

♋

I have had only one uncomfortable contact with my daughter. Four months after her death as I sat one evening watching a DVD, my stomach got queasy, and I suddenly felt a strange restlessness. The formerly engaging film lost its appeal. By its end I felt edgy and upset, as if I might be coming down with the flu. I went to bed quickly. Before my head had fully sunk into the pillow, I could feel Randi yanking at me. She came with so much commotion, I almost felt afraid. Her words tumbled over one another in a jumble. All I could understand was that she was being shown some aspect of her former life that she was not happy about. Very firmly I told her I was sure there were beings where she was who were much more capable of helping her than I was. I directed my daughter back to the land of the dead, and the moment she left, my stomach and mood settled.

I slept well and dreamed of sleeping entwined in a woman's arms. In the morning Randi calmly made her usual visit as if the previous one had been no different than any other. I could not ignore it, though. I asked, "Can I do something to help?" She replied, Would you hold me please? We lay entwined in my bed as in my dream, while I smoothed her hair and kissed her forehead. We spoke about life's challenges and of her mistakes and regrets and of my own. It was a particularly intimate and satisfying contact, the only time I have ever felt as though she had physical substance. Had I not turned away from her and sent her back, I'm sure the contact would have turned more frightening. This gratifying experience was a dramatic demonstration of the positive result of rejecting any contact that disturbs.

❧

Beverly's daughter Myrna was thirty-nine. While caring for her ten-year-old granddaughter, Beverly became so anxious she dashed over to Myrna's home, where she found a hose running, Myrna's lunch waiting on the counter, but no Myrna. She called the police. Together they found Myrna's body outside on her property. How she came to die was never confirmed. Soon Beverly began to experience Myrna's constant presence. There were occasional loving contacts, but most of the time her daughter seemed angry. Things fell off shelves for no reason. There were unexplained loud noises. A heavy chandelier swayed back and forth, especially as Beverly spoke about Myrna. Was Myrna angry about how she had died? Was she upset because she wanted to be there for her daughter? Beverly had no answers. Her only avenue for healing connection was to send love and to pray for her daughter's release into the light, which she did over and over again.

After eighteen months of this, as Beverly sat praying for Myrna with a person she called her "spiritual guru," this guru became aware of the presence of both Myrna and Mother Mary, who was there to escort Myrna across. Myrna, however, was not about to go easily; she had a proviso. ("My daughter was a very powerful woman," Beverly told me.) Myrna, with the guru's help, negotiated with Mother Mary. Myrna did not want the addiction issues she had inherited from her father to pass to her daughter. I won't go unless I can take that darkness with me, was her demand.

Mother Mary told her, "This is not yours to do," but Myrna would not back down. Eventually it was Mother Mary who relented; Myrna's condition was met. Beverly was fully aware of the precise moment in which her daughter completed crossing over into death. Though she had prayed for this moment for a year and a half, it was heartrending. Sensing her daughter cross over felt like a second death. After all those months of sending love and prayers to her daughter, once she enlisted the support of someone capable of helping Myrna move on, the disturbing contacts ceased. After that Beverly and her granddaughter received only benign and loving contacts.

On New Year's Eve Beverly and her granddaughter got all gussied up and were about to take a photo. They invited Myrna. In the photo Myrna appears as a sphere of light. "We invited her to be with us, and there she was. I do believe it is so much simpler than we think," Beverly told me.

Sometimes Beverly and her granddaughter share olfactory visitations where Myrna floods a square yard area with one of her favorite floral scents. Each spontaneous aromatherapy session lasts about three minutes, and they always feel restored by this connection. The shadow side has evolved into something quite lovely and healing.

∾

In Beverly's situation the change to loving contacts after her daughter was supported to cross over made the effect of that support patently clear. I can make no such comparison because, immediately following Randi's death, I called my spiritual counselor. She did her work before I was ever aware of contact with Randi. My situation and Beverly's are the only ones I'm aware of where experts were called upon. Both deaths were sudden; Randi's was suicide, but it was never determined how Myrna died. These stories illustrate the significance of what many who can see and work directly with the dead suggest, that it is best to get expert help for those who have died in violent or sudden manners. These people urge us to be sure such experts come highly recommended, since there are no accreditations for this field. We can rely only on personal recommendations and our own inner guidance. Sometimes we can turn to our religious and spiritual organizations and their leaders for assistance. Many of these, though there are exceptions, have specific rituals, prayers, and practices to benefit the souls of the deceased, such as the Jewish Kaddish, the Greek Orthodox Trisagion, and the rosaries, masses, and novenas of the Catholic Church. My research indicates however, that given time, those stuck between the worlds will be released even without such help. You may recall Donnie, the young musician who visited his friend in dreams for a decade before arriving at the "crossroads" and moving on. Most of my interviewees whose beloveds have died in traumatic ways have been visited in deeply satisfying manners without benefit of expert help. Some of the dead have returned in a few weeks, others in months or even years. It is a splendid gift to get assistance to ensure a beloved's rapid transition. But if this has not been done, there may be no cause for concern, unless ongoing uncomfortable contacts indicate the need for trained assistance.

Another factor that can transform the troubling into something of benefit is to ask ourselves why the dead have engaged with us as they have. Did Celeste's husband's choice to return as a disembodied head indicate some aspect of their relationship that only she would comprehend? Why did Randi come to me with her life review? Her parenting seemed to trouble her the most, and the next day offered me the opportunity to examine aspects of my own parenting and share them with her. This put us on more equal footing as two imperfect mothers. When we seek meaning beneath the surface of a contact, not assuming its nature is merely coincidental, we may uncover its deeper gift.

℘

Our culture has two conflicting misperceptions about ghosts and about hauntings. One is the media's tendency to amplify their frightening aspects. The second misperception appears more benign on the surface. I have stayed in charming old hotels and bed-and-breakfasts where resident ghosts are played up as attractions. Guests are invited to evening talks about the history of ghostly sightings and encouraged to share whatever strange shenanigans they themselves have seen, to add to the lore. My dear friend moved into the very old house her new husband had previously bought and renovated. He bragged that the original section had once been a bar, hinting at the presence of ghosts. I offered, through my friend, who was ill-at-ease in her new home, to see if there were any disembodied beings sharing it or if professional help was needed. I felt particular concern about who might still be hanging around from the bar. My friend's husband refused my offer. He liked the romance of living in a haunted house.

Historical museums often attract the dead. On a nighttime visit, my photographer interviewee has seen numerous glowing orbs zooming around a Clayton, New Mexico, museum. The security system camera showed them clearly, though her camera did not pick them up. Atchison bills itself as "the most haunted town in Kansas"—again the hapless ghost as tourist attraction. Historical buildings and the items within such places may hold and attract some of the dead who were connected to them in life, who are left to haunt the locations like circus sideshow acts, instead of the lost souls they really are.

To those who can see or work with or assist the dead, this approach lacks compassion. Dead beings who still wander the halls of their homes or haunt their saloons are lost between the lands of the living and the dead and in need of assistance to move on. The disembodied have different tasks than the embodied and different places to be. In times and cultures where psychopomp work was common, where it was known that help is often needed for the transition out of this life, I suspect there were many fewer such hauntings. For the most part we live and die now without benefit of such help, yet thousands of people die suddenly each year on our highways alone. There is always war someplace on the globe; murder and suicide rates are high. If, as is so for many modern people, we do not trust that consciousness continues after death, the fact that we *do* still exist may hold us back, because we won't believe we are no longer alive. Unaware of Spirit's compassionate nature, we may be terrified of being punished for mistakes we've made in our lives.

If the newly dead merely float on the river that runs between the realms, they are neither here nor there. They remind me of high school students who cut class to hang out behind the schoolyard, smoking and passing around bottles of cheap booze. Such bored and unfocused teenagers sometimes end up causing calamity. In this way the dead may also create havoc. The way to both protect ourselves and support the dead is to send them our loving prayers and reject anything that is less than fully satisfying.

Chapter Seven

NOTHING CAN TOUCH
IT OR TAKE IT AWAY

Words are nets through which all truth escapes.
—*Paula Fox*, News from the World

In Japanese culture it is considered of vital importance to visit one's ancestral graves. When Yuki flew to Japan at age twenty-four with her American mother and Japanese father, they took her Great-Aunt Akiko by train for this honoring process. At a Buddhist temple in the tiny village of Saijo a monk invited them in for tea and offered to perform an Obon, or Ancestor Ceremony. Yuki had been to Ancestor Ceremonies as a child in the States, but in Japan this ceremony was more impactful. Her Japanese was limited; she could not understand the monk's incantations, and she had no particular expectations. Yet, as the monk prayed and the incense swirled and mingled with the sunlight, her senses heightened, her awareness expanded, and she could sense—not see, yet feel—the innumerable loving presences of her ancestors as they arrived. As the rite unfolded, she grew more and more convinced that every one of her Japanese ancestors was present and that they would always stand behind her. She felt filled to the brim with their support. Tangibly, as the monk began his closing prayers, her ancestors ebbed away, and her awareness returned to its everyday state. Twenty-four years later, still conscious of that ancestral underpinning, her face shone with the memory of it.

As Yuki finished her story I could feel Randi's tingling presence arrive with force in my body. She punctuated Yuki's story by adding, Yes, yes, this is how it is. If you invite us, we will come, and we will support you. She seemed to include herself with the ancestors, so perhaps we can define ancestor as anyone who predeceases us. Although most of the experiences I have heard illustrate times when the dead have come of their own accord, this Ancestor Ceremony and my daughter's reaction to it show us that we can be more proactive. Recently Yuki gave me a tour of the new section she had added to her massage spa to better accommodate elderly and disabled clients. Like an ancient guardian, an oil painting by her Japanese grandfather dominates one wall of the reception area. This painting honors her ancestral support by making it visible to all who enter.

❧

Dr. Lynn, as he is most often called, took that more proactive stance in several ways with his father. Their relationship had been neither intimate nor supportive. As a child, if he fell asleep in his father's lap, his father would touch him affectionately, but the moment Lynn showed signs of awakening, he'd stop, as if embarrassed to show his love. In Dr. Lynn's adulthood, when his father came for a three-day visit, he'd leave in two before there was any chance for the close connection his son yearned for. Lynn went to college on a hockey scholarship. His father dreamed of him becoming a hockey star, but this was not Lynn's dream. No matter what his accomplishments—and they were many, including a PhD (hence the "Dr." Lynn)—his father's pride was always stained by a hint of disappointment.

As his father neared death, Dr. Lynn visited in the hospital, suggesting they simply "be totally present" together. They held hands for a blissful half hour, looking into one another's eyes. Afterward, a radiant Dr. Lynn strode past the nurses' station with tears streaming. A worried nurse stopped him to ask, "What's happened?"

"I've just had the best goodbye any son could have with his father," he replied. A month or so later as he lay in bed, half-awake, half-asleep, his father appeared in what Dr. Lynn called a hypnagogic dream. He told me, "We had a great time together, but very quickly my dad said, 'I have to go now.'"

"Dad, you do this all the time. Remember how it was in the hospital?" His dad stayed; their connection deepened.

"I have to go now."

"You can feel how juicy this is. Can't you stay?" His dad stayed; the connection got even more loving.

"Now I *really* have to go."

"Okay, Dad, at least we have this." He fell asleep. He was awakened by a call from his mother; his father had died at precisely the time when their connection had occurred. Thanks to his persistence, they had achieved a new level of intimacy both prior to his father's death and at the moment of his death. Decades passed. Dr. Lynn retired and began to write books on consciousness. His yearning for more connection and support from his father stayed alive. Eventually he asked in meditation to contact his father, and his father came. "I could use some help with my work," Lynn said. Dr. Lynn told me his father's presence seemed diffuse and vague, though the connection was still rich. His father thanked him for finding me, for making this request. I never knew what you wanted. Now I do, and now I will be supportive.

I hear the echo of Randi's words, If you invite us, we will come. Dr. Lynn was unwilling to accept less than what he longed for, even if it took thirty-five years to culminate in this contact. He views this as part of our task as human beings—to make peace with our ancestors and to ask for their support. Once we ourselves have died, it may be one of our tasks to give that support. While we live, we can make it unequivocally clear to the deceased just what it is we want and need, grounding ourselves in our familial DNA, keeping alive a resource that is often ignored as impossible to access.

ev

Tom asked for ancestral love and support in another manner. His father too had not been one to express love or affection, and their relationship troubled Tom long after his father's death. When Tom's wife returned from studying *curanderia* (a form of Latin American traditional healing) in Mexico with Dr. Arturo Ornelas, she taught her husband a Maya ceremony for reconnecting with his father and healing their relationship. He prepared a burial mound with dirt and stones, where he could see the sunset. She instructed him to visit this mound for nine consecutive days at sunset, bringing rose petals, water, a candle, and a photo or other memorabilia. Tom selected a stern and formal photo of his lawyer dad. Each evening he spread rose petals over the mound and sprinkled water in the four cardinal directions to honor and include them. He lit the candle, and as he stood facing the setting sun, he addressed his father. On the second and third days, his father appeared to smile in this serious photo. On the fourth day, Tom could feel his father's presence and sense his father's love. On the fifth day and each subsequent day, Tom and his father held conversations.

"For the first time I knew just how much my father loved me," he told me, crying as he spoke. He broke into a smile and continued, "I always cry when I speak of this ceremony. It healed my entire relationship with my father." He said that after the ninth day, still following instructions, he had dismantled the mound and placed the dirt and stones around a tree in order to use it as a place to visit his father and honor him in an annual ceremony; his wife had told him he could also use this soil to plant a tree to serve the same purpose.

૯૦

Rosalie's relationship with her husband Miles did not need healing after his death. "Even after forty-one years of marriage," she said, "he could still surprise me."

When he was eighty-seven and dying of lung cancer, Rosalie reassured him, "You don't have to stay for me. I can cope, if you will be my guardian angel."

"If I can, I will," he had promised. Another time, he teased, "I'm going to be everywhere, even under your bed."

Miles kept his promise in ways all across the ADC spectrum. There were electronic malfunctions, physical manipulations, synchronous experiences, and seven surprising moon appearances, like having clouds swirl, not across the face of the moon but, impossibly, behind it. Of course, Miles had known how much Rosalie loved the moon and "all things celestial," so these particular moments felt like a touch from him through the heavens. During his illness, because of his need to sleep in the daytime, they had installed eight remote-controlled shades over the eight clerestory windows above the bed. On the night of his death she pushed ALL on the remote, which she had done many times before. On this occasion though, only seven shades lowered, with the full moon centered in the eighth window. It was so soon after his death, she was not yet sure Miles had done this, but she thanked him, just in case. Lying on the bathroom counter, her cell phone suddenly flashed his cell phone number. She called her computer guru. No matter what way she explained the particulars of her last phone usage, he told her this number appearing as it had was "not possible," adding, "Miles must have done it."

A favorite ring of her husband's, other objects she couldn't find, would magically appear in obvious places like on her nightstand whenever she asked Miles for help finding them. She asked for his help selecting memorabilia for his memorial service and was led to a ten-year-old love letter from one of the few times they had ever been apart. He had written, "We never have to be sad when we're not together physically, because it doesn't matter. We are still together and always will be. It's a good thought to keep in mind." These frequent signs, twenty-nine in all in the first six months alone (she tracked them on her phone), convinced her this was Miles letting her know he was everywhere, no doubt even under the bed. Rosalie invited Miles and thanked him. He came, and he continues to come.

ℰᴗ

Rita's marriage was not so pacific, and her husband died at age fifty-five, not at eighty-seven as Miles had, leaving her with three children at home and a working farm to run. Her preparation for his sudden death by heart attack had begun two years earlier with a fervent prayer to Jesus for support with dealing with her husband's temper. This was followed by a series of intense "bad" dreams about his death that included one of standing beside his flag-draped coffin. Because of these dreams, Rita urged him repeatedly to visit a doctor, but he refused. So Rita set the dreams aside. After his death she discovered that each of their three children had also been having "bad" dreams about their father's death.

Two nights post-death, Rita's husband appeared to her in their hallway, shadowy, yet with clearly delineated facial features. He told her, I just came to say hi. As she walked toward him, he said, You can't touch me. It hasn't been long enough. Rita says he checked in many times like this, and the children often felt his presence too. Numerous vivid dreams continued for all four of them. At times Rita could smell and taste him in her dreams, as if they were making love. There were visual visitations, and what Rita described as a "chill" up her left arm.[1] Once, the whole family shared a visitation. The children were all participating in a school concert. In the audience, Rita was feeling especially lonely among all the couples and families, when she sensed him sitting down in the empty seat beside her, as though this place had been saved for him. From the stage, all three children saw their father as a shadow entering through the gym's double doors.

Visitations and dreams continued for them all over several years. Rita stressed to me what a healing and a teaching these various contacts were, not only for her, but also for the children and for them as a family. After a few years she had a lush blue and green dream with flowers and trees and a beautiful bridge over a small, deep river, "like a joyful and well-maintained park." The bridge came with the crystal clear awareness that "to cross it was to not return." Her husband was not in this dream, which she understood to mean that a certain level of healing between them had been concluded. She need not go there with him anymore.

Rita says her husband's death opened her to a journey of deep exploration and healing of her current and past lives. The concept of reincarnation, that we live more than one life, that we have been more than this personality, this body in which we now exist, is an ancient one, and I delve into it further in my next chapter. Rita says their after-death contact gave the couple a thirty-year opportunity to "heal their karmic issues on a soul level." Sometimes there was anger between them when he visited; sometimes she "sent him to the light" and shut him out. She took the final step in this healing through a spiritual practice designed to complete connection with a deceased beloved. This practice began with listing the good in their life together. She told me that twelve days into this she sensed that he had "left for good." When I did the math that he had died at age fifty-five and visited for thirty more years, I was intrigued to note that he and Rita had stayed linked until he was nearly the age at which Rosalie's husband Miles had died. Here is another marriage that continued, long after death.

ও

Dana's connections with her daughter Joy, after Joy's death, have been many and varied. Joy was not yet nineteen when she tried black tar heroin. Her friends, perhaps less fragile than she, survived this experiment, but Joy was "pale, shy, slight, troubled by the state of the world," and for her the dose was fatal. As Dana hugged one of her other daughters the morning after Joy's death, they spoke of hints of fore-knowledge. Her daughter said she had always known she would lose a sister. Dana conceded for the first time that she too had felt this possibility. Joy had been the daughter who worried her most. In this moment she felt Joy lift this weight of concern from her shoulders, saying as she did so, You don't have to worry about me anymore, Mom.

Later, at a Buddhist Vipassana meditation retreat, Dana was replaying what she might have done differently as a mother, when she felt a slight pressure on her temples. She heard a voice say within her, Make peace with this, Mom. It's not your fault. As these words were spoken, the pressure released. Dana told me it was the pressure and its release that confirmed for her that the words had come from her daughter, that they were not a product of her own mind's attempt to reassure itself. The dead love to help us address how easily we humans look for fault and accept the weight of blame. Joy has often visited her mother and others in subtle ways, with a touch on the hand, a sense of her sitting nearby. Dana experienced her once as a "dark rainbow, an iridescent light" that disappeared if she looked at it directly. As if to help Dana with any doubts about these contacts, as she looked through a shelf at the library, a book on visitations from the dead fell off at her feet. Reading it confirmed what she had already known was real.

In one of her daughter's journals Dana found a complex drawing Joy had done at about age ten. This drawing conveys several elements related to Joy's death: the sombrero-clad Mexican who had sold the heroin; the sleeping bag in which she had died, with a skeletal head emerging from it; the dog park she and her friends had been camping in when she died. Alone, these images might have only confused and disturbed Dana, but the upper part of the drawing, with its repeated and increasingly joyous faces rising up into the sky with a sense of release, brings her comfort. We are left with more questions though. What can we do with this idea that a child of ten could have foreknowledge—we assume less than conscious—of her own death that would not occur for eight more years?

The next experience reveals again this pattern that those of us with the most tragic life situations often experience the most uplifting connections after death. I hope that the sweet taste of these healings is not soured by the bitterness of the tales that provoked them, since the stories show how we are supported in the midst of the most pain life has to offer. At our café interview, Lorraine struck me as a resilient, lively, loving woman with the strength to face life's difficulties head-on and to grow through them. The series of connections both before and after her siblings' deaths acknowledges a bond of love that transcends the family's physical and emotional trials.

As a backstory, Lorraine began by relating their mother's mental illness and their father's abuse. The three siblings had been estranged for a long time. Shortly before depression drove her brother to take his own life, he came to visit her for the first time in many years. Two weeks after his death, Lorraine awoke from an unsettling dream of him. As if to balance both the dream and their long years of separation, he appeared to her as clearly as though he were still alive, lounging against her bedroom doorjamb. She did what we all seem to do when we see a vision in our bedrooms, glanced over to see if her husband could see it, too. He was sleeping soundly. She addressed her brother aloud, "Is that you?"

He put a finger to his lips. Shhh, I'm okay, he whispered and faded away as her husband slept on. Visions, like dreams, are most often private affairs.

A dozen years later Lorraine discovered that her sister was deathly ill and forging prescriptions to obtain drugs. Lorraine gained legal guardianship and cared for her until her death. Two months later Lorraine dreamed of her. She still looked dreadful, disheveled and dirty, only now she was in the shower. As she bathed, her entire body was washed down the drain. When she emerged, she was red-haired and lovely, as she had once been. I am so sorry, she said to Lorraine. Anyone who has ever had trouble sleeping after a violent film can attest to the persistence of images, to how they can replay their horror behind closed eyelids. They can also adhere to us like glue following a death, but in both these after-death contacts Lorraine's memory was restored with beautiful visuals and a sense that her siblings' anguish had been eased, that they were continuing to progress and to transform after death.

∽

All those people who spoke with me about their visual experiences attended with great care to their choice of words. They each seemed frustrated by the inadequacy of language to reveal the radiant power and true nature of what they had seen and experienced. I kept hearing oddly redundant adjectives: "a pure, pure white light" or "the purest of white, white lights." I wanted to clean up these repetitions, to paraphrase, not to quote, until I came to realize how incapable the English language is of describing the essence of a transcendent experience. Everyone's tones and expressions revealed their dissatisfaction with even their "white, white" repetitions as they said these phrases twice more within three minutes.

The most lavish description I heard was of the rainbow Diane saw the day after her mother's death, stretched straight across the sky, from horizon to horizon. "It was glorious, wildly dramatic, outrageous, the most unbelievably extravagant rainbow. What a show! My whole range of vision was beautiful with light and color." Diane felt that her mother, who had been a painter, had created this rainbow for her as a gift.

ᆳ

No one seemed more frustrated with the limitations of the English language than my first husband Bob, the father of my two daughters, when describing his contact with Randi. Bob had called to thank me for a package of photos of Randi I had copied and sent him. How I came to have these photos is an ADC story all its own. Years ago, when Randi was in high school and college, Bob had lived with a woman I will call Heidi. Heidi and I had been friends, but after I moved away, we had lost touch. She had no way to know of Randi's death, when suddenly one day she felt an overwhelming awareness of Randi's presence. Heidi told me there had been "no memory trigger," that the feeling was "out of the ordinary," and something she "could not dismiss." This compelled her to go online, where she first was shocked to find Randi's obituary and, with some diligence, was eventually able to reconnect with me. One result of this was that Heidi sent me a box of Randi's high school memorabilia—horse show ribbons, newspaper clippings about her successes, and photos—that Bob had inadvertently left behind when he and Heidi had separated nearly thirty years earlier.

Now Bob and I were speaking on the phone, not a common occurrence. He did not yet know I was writing this book. Inspired by what I had shared about Heidi's contact in the note accompanying the photos, he told me of his contact with Randi. Our conversation was taking place nearly three years after the fact, but the wonder in his voice was fresh. "I was asleep," he told me, "but I was not dreaming." This was a new state of consciousness to him, and with his long relationship with the metaphysical he is no stranger to other states of consciousness. He said they had met someplace *beyond* dreams and he did not know how to describe where they were except to say, "It was like being in the middle of eternity." I'm sure he used that phrase—in the middle of eternity—three times. This place was entirely lit by a "luminous, Milky Way light." She looked to be about twenty and was very, very beautiful. She too was emitting luminous light that glowed from within her and blended into the luminosity that surrounded them both. They did not speak. "No words were needed," Bob said. Bathed by this exquisite light, my dead daughter and her father held one another for a very long time. "She was so beautiful," he repeated.

He likened leaving this experience to the reverse of waking from a dream. He repeated that he was on the other side of dreaming, and he had to "come down" into the normal dream-state from where they had been. As he shared this, I cried at how perfect it is that Randi has come to both her parents in such satisfying and distinctly unique ways. How perfect it is that Randi's contact with Heidi had made it possible for me to hear of Bob's experience and that he was allowing me to share it in this book. How perfect it is that Randi has reconnected me with this old friend and that my granddaughter Chelsey now owns these important items from her mother's past. The whole family now has these photos from a happy time in Randi's life. How perfect it is that Randi has facilitated all this healing by her various contacts.

℘

Marcia was my next-door neighbor for a decade when we both lived in California. Almost as soon as she heard I was writing this book, she sent me the story of what had occurred after her brother took his own life. She said she had cried for days, that her head ached from her effort to understand. In an attempt to ease both her aching heart and her aching head, she walked and walked, alone in a nearby park, where I used to walk, too. I recall the old quarry, where walkers had carefully placed rocks into a labyrinth. This quarry seemed to have its own vortex, as though spirit were more accessible there, and it drew Marcia into it. She sat down, closed her eyes, and was washed over with peacefulness. She could feel her brother Ken's presence surrounding her. He seemed to be everywhere, and when she opened her eyes, he *was* everywhere. He sat facing her, and yet he also sat to either side of her. There were ten of him, ten versions, ten replicas of her brother, ten Kens sitting cross-legged as she was, in a circle, each with both his arms extended, hands resting and spreading over the back of each of the other versions of himself. The arms of the brothers to her immediate right and left embraced her. I am okay, he assured her, and again, I am okay, as he touched her and gazed into her eyes. She told me this level of comfort and reassurance was so far beyond anything she could ever have hoped for, that "nothing can touch it or take it from me," that now she knows something about the afterlife she had only guessed about before.

The nature of a direct experience like this is that it is irrefutable to the one who has it. We live surrounded by a sea of facts: books, magazines, newspapers, radio, television, computers, the Internet, Wikipedia, signs, ads, billboards, the bumper sticker on the car ahead of us, corporations, religions. These all have something to tell us or sell us or prove. Our dashboards inform us of temperature, inside and out, time, miles per hour, and miles per gallon. All of this information is put forth as fact, yet how many of these facts are irrefutable? Yesterday I watched an "infallible" atomic clock vacillate between Daylight Savings Time and Standard. The study that is touted on the front page in one year is exposed as flawed in the next. Randi told me writing this book would transform me, and it is the irrefutable aspect of our contact and of hearing about these other contacts that has done so. These have taught me to trust my own direct, mystical experience above all else, for the mystical has no ulterior motive. If it has any agenda at all, it is to support our growth and well-being, nothing more.

&

As soon as we met for our interview, Natalie told me she had already discussed the issue of whether to contribute to this book with both her husband Nelson and their deceased friend Kelly's husband. They had all agreed it was no invasion of Kelly's privacy to share this experience; they hoped including it here would show others the beauty that after-death communication can bring. Their dear friend Kelly had been pregnant with her first child when she developed a blood clot and died in the ambulance on the way to the hospital. When Nelson's grandfather died on the same day and the scheduling of the funerals did not allow them both to attend both services, the couple divided forces. Nelson had already committed to being one of Kelly's pallbearers, so he asked Natalie to represent him at his grandfather's funeral. She agreed, though this choice was difficult and distressing for her, and after the funerals Natalie remained sad and uneasy.

A few days later, lying beside Nelson in bed, she prayed to God to deliver her goodbyes and her gratitude for their friendship to Kelly. Her body was slowly enveloped by warmth that began in her toes and surged all the way up through her head. She felt safe, as though wrapped in the warmest of blankets. "A bright ray of pure white light appeared" and in the center a brilliant oval framed Kelly's smiling face and upper body. "Since I'm a detailer in my artwork," Natalie said, "I took in every detail. She was clothed in a pure white gown and the lighting that surrounded her head radiated a soft glow. She was smiling . . . and at peace." Natalie began to cry. Kelly spoke. It's okay, Natalie, I'm home now.

"I whispered my goodbyes and she slowly faded away." The light and the warmth dissipated, Nelson still sleeping unaware beside her. Natalie is a devout Catholic. She says this answer to her prayer strengthened her faith, showed her that "God is with me," and helped her to lose her fear of death. Later, as Natalie shared this vision with Kelly's husband, he interrupted her to describe his wife exactly as Natalie had seen her. She had come to him as well, said she loved him, and given him one final hug.

I was affected by the integrity and love in how these friends considered Kelly's feelings about their participation in this book. Some other interviewees also took their dead beloveds' feelings into account when they shared with me or reviewed my notes. One who had originally said I could use her and her husband's full names, changed her mind when she recalled him once saying that our names should only be in the paper at birth and at death. Another felt her husband would have been uncomfortable with an intimate detail she had shared and asked me not to include it.

☙❧

Nora's experiences span the five years between a pregnancy in which her son Shannon was stillborn and when her daughter Jody was about seventeen months old. Between Nora's pregnancies she had frequently sensed Shannon's presence. Nora is positive, and an intensely disturbing dream reinforced her conviction, that she had carried twins during the earlier pregnancy and had resorbed a daughter back into her body through a phenomenon she later learned is called "vanishing twin syndrome." Jody knew that her brother Shannon had died before she was born.

She was three and a half when I sat between her and her mother for our interview. The story was mostly Jody's, but she was shy with me and munched on a snack and drew, nodding occasionally as her mother told me that when Jody was first able to verbalize, she awoke one day, saying someone was with her, pointing at the ceiling light, and asking to be lifted up to touch it. She inserted her hand between its lights in a pattern, appearing to play with a companion. Most striking was how her eyes shone with love. Nora had no idea what this was about, but after a few similar times, she thought to ask Jody if this playmate was Shannon. Jody said it was and after that she used his name. Sometimes she would sob and say, "Shannon go away" (she had not yet mastered past tense), or giggle and say, "Shannon funny," or "Shannon, bed, snuggle, nap." Incidents like this occurred regularly for more than a month. Nora wonders if Jody could be the twin her body had resorbed. At the end of our interview, Jody gave me what she had been drawing. It was two circles, joined by yellow lines. Jody and her stillborn twin brother, I wondered?

Vicki, a woman who had miscarried as her grandmother lay dying, described how her grandmother would almost die, then rally, then touch death again. Her grandmother knew nothing of Vicki's pregnancy or of her miscarriage, yet, returning from one of her brushes with death, she said excitedly, "I saw your baby! I want to know her name. She's beautiful."

∞

As I heard more ADC experiences, patterns of gender difference began to appear. You may have noticed that most of my interviews (around 80 percent) have been with women. Those men who did share with me were as open and communicative as the women have been. Have there been so few men, because men tend to be less comfortable with the mystical, more so with the rational? Or are they simply less comfortable with talking about the mystical with a stranger, particularly with a woman? After death, this pattern changes. The dead who have made contact have been almost equally divided between males and females; there have been a few more men although not enough to be notable. What *is* notable is the number of men who either return unbidden or, as in the cases of Dr. Lynn and Tom with their fathers, were invoked to return to heal flawed relationships.

When neglect, abuse, or suffering has stained an entire relationship, death can leave behind a wake of tears laced with blood that will not clot. Two violently cruel fathers returned in dreams so transformed their daughters told me their whole relationships with them were transfigured and replaced, yet I can share neither dream. One woman felt the healing was so complete she didn't want to place any emphasis on the destructiveness of their former relationship. The second woman, who said she had been wholly able to forgive her disturbed and alcoholic father in a single, powerful dream, later withdrew permission to share it, though another experience of hers is in another chapter.

ꙮ

Vicki had no such compunction. She was eager to have her tale included here. It was she, not her abusive grandfather, who had sought out healing. Though Vicki herself had been protected from him, she described him as a "dedicated pedophile" and eventually a convicted one, who sexually abused many people both outside of and within her family, including Vicki's mother. Vicki told me she was brought up to hate her grandfather and that "we wore this hatred like a badge." He died when she was sixteen, a cause for family celebration. Yet Vicki could not forget that he had "fathered my mom, who is definitely a human angel and one of the most important beings in my world."

Ten years later, as she developed spiritually, she could no longer tolerate the double-pointed knife of her hatred for him. She had come to understand how much hatred harms the one who hates. She enlisted the aid of a woman she described as an "angel communicator" with psychic capabilities. Vicki asked her for help in "anchoring my forgiveness in the spirit-world." The woman located Vicki's weeping grandfather in a "self-imposed hell of shame," surrounded by others who suffered in the same manner. When he was given Vicki's message of forgiveness, the medium saw Jesus (her grandfather's face for the divine, Vicki said) appear within a light and also forgive him. Vicki's grandfather stepped out of his hell as a man transformed and reached back to tell others they too were forgiven, releasing them in what Vicki called a "chain reaction of love." She says she has never again felt hatred toward her grandfather.

I once received an inner teaching during meditation on the superfluousness of the verb to forgive. I was told that to forgive someone is simply to restore the natural state of unconditional love between us that has, for whatever reason, been set aside. That the enormity of this man's abuse could be undone by a single act of restoring love is beyond my ken. Surely each of those he had abused must also make their peace with him. Yet this experience reflects the restorative possibilities built into the after-death state, as well as demonstrating another path the living can use to connect with their dead beloveds.

ↀ

At the time that Helena and I spoke, on a summer afternoon beneath the shade of my juniper trees, I did not yet realize how much I would hear about after-death healing with men, especially with fathers. Helena told me if she had had any idea she would have after-death contact with one of her parents, she would have expected it to be with her mother. They had been close, with few unresolved issues remaining between them. Helena's relationship with her father was not troubled, or even difficult, just not well-developed, due to his reserved nature.

He came to her first in a dream that she described as "more like an experience, like a contact, than a dream." She sat amid the quiet buzz of a filled auditorium, awaiting a performance, and discovered her father in the seat beside her. He had two forms. He was himself, human-sized, perhaps forty-five years old (though he had been much older at his death), with apple-round cheeks. Simultaneously, he was a huge, white mountain. She felt ecstatic in his presence and aware that his true form was the mountain, though he needed his human form so she could recognize him. He told her, There is no need to worry about anything concerning me. Then he added, There is no need to worry about anything. She calls this dream experience a "referent." If she feels worried or sad or frightened or confused, she returns to his words, which still carry "fragrance. They remind me that the nature of life is joy."

Helena's family is musical, and certain music always invokes her father's memory. As she was driving the thirty miles from her mountain home into town, a full day of errands and appointments ahead of her, she popped in a CD of her father's favorite, Handel's *Messiah*. He seemed to accompany her as she sang along to the "Hallelujah Chorus." It felt sweet and satisfying to know her father was somehow with her. It became less sweet and satisfying once she arrived in town. Should she turn left or right? Why was it she had come to town anyway? Everything and every place confused her. With considerable effort, she located a café, where she found that at least relating to people was easy and normal. She ordered hot tea and opened her journal: she could write one sentence, but when she got to the next, she couldn't recall the first. Suddenly fearful, she wondered if this loss of cognitive ability could be a symptom of a stroke or something gone haywire in her body. She turned her attention to her heart; it seemed to be working just fine. Then she realized how absolutely marvelous she felt. It was only that her left, logical brain had abandoned her.

There was something wondrous about whatever was happening, so she didn't want to close it off, yet how was she to function? Surely this had to do with her father, the music, and their singing together. "Dad," she said to him, "I have to learn to live in two worlds." Nothing changed; she still could scarcely think. She struggled to maneuver her way through what she hoped were the most crucial of her commitments. She arrived at her appointment to tutor a student, at the right place and at the right hour—an accomplishment in itself—and abandoned her written plan and improvised verbally. At her acupuncturist's she sighed with relief, able at last to lie down. She described her condition. The treatment restored her to her rationality and grounded her in the physical world. What remained was an ecstatic state of oneness, pure joy, freedom, and celebration, a conviction that it would be her father who would meet her at death's door when her time came.

This day viscerally confirmed what she thought she had already known, that we exist within simultaneous realities. Helena told me in her poetic way that the day is a "live memory of an aerated life." In combination with the dream of her father as a white mountain, the day "replaced everything in our relationship; this is what is true about him." She did not use the word "support," as Dr. Lynn and others have done, yet as she shared the strength of this experience it was obvious that her father's presence and his powerful support were now concretely embodied within her. Death, so often viewed as the closing of a door, as a loss of opportunity, at times enlarges the opening between two people, freeing the dead from the constraints of their earthbound personalities.

Chapter Eight

TO WHAT END?

*I could not bring together the torn ragged edges of God's
love and suffering . . .*
—*Christine Sherwood,* Fire & Ash: The Alchemy of Cancer

The brush with the divine that after-death communication brings can enhance our work or move us toward our
true calling. Certain work, particularly hands-on touch and
energy-healing techniques and being with the dying and the
bereaved, opens its practitioners to receiving after-death contact, either to assist them or their clients. Sometimes ADC
experiences can influence many, remedying much more than
the immediate grief of the single living person who had the
contact. Authors Wendy Jordan (*Embracing the End-of-Life
Journey*) and Denys Cope (*Dying, a Natural Passage*) both
work with the dying. Denys' book emerged from decades
at the bedsides of the dying, first in hospice and later in a
business in which she manages the myriad needs of dying
people. She told me she has heard hundreds of ADC stories

from her clients and their families, though what she shared with me were two of her own experiences.

Because his nursing home roommate said her brother had cried out at the moment of death, Denys kept worrying about him. That night, like the clock in the nursery rhyme that "stopped short, never to go again," the family's heirloom grandfather clock stopped at 11:10. Denys thought, *That's not surprising. After all, it's a very old clock.* The clock was reset. At exactly 11:10 the next night, it stopped again. She tried to parse meaning from the time without success; her brother had died in the early morning. Again, the clock was reset. The third night that the clock stopped at 11:10, Denys got the message. Sitting on the same couch where she'd been on the night of her father's death fifteen years earlier, she recalled that it was he who had died at 11:10 PM. She now felt this was her father telling her that her brother was with him, so she need not worry. The clock, which had never stopped before those three nights, has not stopped since.

Denys had a client who had been a chiropractor, a man she described as highly spiritual and the only patient she's ever had who wanted to spend most of their time together in silence. His hospice nurse told Denys she had played The Beatles' "Yellow Submarine" on his boom box as she washed his body after his death. I don't know whether this was a favorite song of his or maybe of hers. Whatever her reasons for playing it, it appears he did hear the music because of what happened to Denys a few days later. She lay with closed eyes receiving a bodywork treatment when she distinctly felt three comforting hands—one on her feet, another on her belly, a third on her forehead. This was so improbable, Denys opened her eyes to take a peek. As she saw that both the bodyworker's hands were fully occupied on feet and belly, "Yellow Submarine" streamed through her mind. At once Denys knew the third hand was her chiropractor client's. At the session's end, the practitioner, who was pregnant and had specifically told Denys she wanted nothing to do with death or dying during her pregnancy, said, "Mine weren't the only hands that were working on you." When Denys told the story of her newly deceased client, suggesting that the other hand was his, it had an immediate and transformational effect. "I guess death is not so bad after all," the woman admitted. She had appreciated working in concert with this man's energy. Because she had been unaware he was deceased, and yet fully aware that his energy was healing, she was able to override her dark view of the dead as beings to be feared.

The other author, Wendy Jordan, first shared an olfactory ADC experience she had had with her father. He had been a professional trumpet player and teacher. As a child she had loved to watch him clean and oil his instrument. The odor of trumpet oil is "neither offensive nor so strong it would permeate the house," she explained, "but it is unique, a little more industrial than olive oil. Nothing else smells like it." So when that smell came to her often for several months after his death at age eighty-one, it unequivocally announced her father's presence.

Wendy specializes in spiritual healing through Reiki[1] treatments for people nearing death and their families. Occasionally she senses when clients pass out of their bodies. She may feel them saying, *Thank you, Wendy,* or a quick and sweet, *I'm okay,* which seems quite similar to Denys Cope's client's touch after death, signs of acknowledgment and gratitude.

It takes a distinctive person to stay present with a family as it goes through the dying and death of a beloved, perhaps most especially when that beloved is very young. Among Wendy's more emotionally challenging clients—though also possibly among the more rewarding due to the intimacy she achieved with his family—was a baby boy with a brain tumor. After his death the family chose what Wendy called the "perfect gravesite" beneath a lovely tree. She sat under this tree beside the boy's mother at his funeral service. As the rabbi spoke, a large and beautiful insect repeatedly flew over and dipped into and out of the open grave. A cemetery worker came over with a shovel to rid them of what he thought must be a terrible distraction. When he raised his shovel, Wendy and the mother both gasped and glared and shook their heads at him; they knew this insect was the baby, checking out his grave and making his presence known for one final time.

℘

Celeste's elderly mother had seemed barely interested in the Reiki treatments Celeste gave her before her death. Some time after her death though, she entered a room where Celeste stood in a circle of practitioners giving treatments to someone lying in the circle's center. Her mother slipped into the empty space beside Celeste. When it was her turn to receive, her mother received, too, informing Celeste, *Now I get it.*

During the first couple of years after my daughter's death, my Reiki practitioner reported working on me and on Randi together in my sessions. Another healer, who works with sound, touch, and energy, asks her inner guides to screen the forces that participate in her sessions to be certain they are supportive ones, and sometimes she too receives messages from the dead. One message had seemed so strange she questioned whether she should share it with her client. Yet when she did so, all the tension and pain in the woman's body instantly released, initiating a process of deep and lasting healing.

℘

Kathleen Matta is a nurse and a nurse educator. Three days after the ceremony to scatter the ashes of her dear friend and fellow nurse Loyce, Kathleen was yanked outside by the raucous caw-caw of six or seven ravens in the cottonwood tree in her courtyard. If you've ever heard this sound, you know that even a single nearby raven can be shockingly loud; a half-dozen ravens inside a courtyard are a cacophony, and this cottonwood had never before drawn anything but songbirds. Kathleen had grown up around Native Americans; knowing they consider ravens to be messengers, she asked the birds, "What's going on?" At the sound of her voice, the ravens lifted up and all flew away but one. She knew this one was her dead friend Loyce, and they began to talk.

"What are you doing?" her husband asked.

"I'm talking to Loyce."

"Right. You're talking to Loyce."

About once a month a group of ravens landed in the cottonwood. When they all flew off but one, Kathleen knew this was Loyce telling her all was fine with her. Kathleen's husband didn't laugh at this, but there was nothing to indicate more than his tolerance either until the morning he excitedly woke her. "Kathleen, you have to get up."

"No, I don't. It's Saturday. I'm not working today."

"You have to get up."

"Why?"

"Loyce is here."

And she was.

When the ravens dragged Kathleen out of bed at 6:30 AM on her thirtieth wedding anniversary, she scolded, "It's too early!" But she was up already (if cranky), and they talked. For several years after this there was no contact, then Loyce renewed her old habit of arriving in the same manner. Kathleen continues to freely share this story of Loyce and the ravens. Nurses who knew Loyce will ask, "Have you heard from Loyce lately?" Kathleen also tells the Loyce story to her students, awakening them to the possibility of ADC. Kathleen hopes in this way to open these nurses in New Mexico, where there are many Native American patients and few Native American nurses, to the cultural variations and beliefs they may encounter with their patients.

The influence on Kathleen's husband has also continued. About a year after his mother's death, one morning he told Kathleen, "Mom came to see me last night. I felt a hand on my face, and it wasn't you." Kathleen's experiences seem a perfect example of how the dead can participate in our work, and particularly of how they nudge us to expose people and teach people about what is possible in contact with the dead. I imagine Loyce as pleased by how the effect of her visitations has rippled out through Kathleen's community, perhaps preparing the path for others besides Kathleen's husband to receive communication from their dead beloveds. Maybe this is why Loyce has continued to visit over such a long period of time. It is a way to encourage Kathleen to keep on talking about these contacts to her family, to her coworkers, and to her students.

∽

These women work with illness and death and dying, but the dead don't limit their career-related support to these fields. On the morning after our father's death, my sister Eve awakened early, aware of an inarguable directive to shower and get on down to the office. The office meant our father's magazine publishing business, where she had worked in her twenties; the business she and I had inherited overnight. As she walked the two blocks there, she felt compelled to hurry, as if pulled by a magnet. *Why am I doing this?* she wondered. She had left me, my husband, and our dear friend Jillis asleep on the living room floor where we had dragged the mattresses the night before. We four adults had slept side by side like children too afraid of the dark to sleep alone. Now, incapable of slowing down, she raced on. At the office, she felt her way around as if dowsing for water, thinking, *I don't know why I'm here, but I'll be here until it gets clear.* Some force pulled her into our father's cluttered space to sit in his chair. She demanded aloud, "What do you want me to find?" The sense of urgency only increased. There was something she needed to do, yet it seemed not to be her own need. "What do you want me to do?" she shouted.

It was our father who answered, saying he wanted her to run this magazine. He didn't want his grand achievement to die with him. Years ago, when she had become the Buyers' Guide editor, he had seen the possibility of passing the magazine on to her. Although she had gained a full appreciation of the field, she had resigned to move across the country. All kinds of thoughts flashed through her while he was showing her that she was the one to do this. In her timeless altered state, she does not know how long she spent balancing in her mind the major shifts and changes that saying yes would require. Finally she replied, "Okay, I'll do it." As she said these words, all urgency sloughed away.

At first glance this might appear to have been a precipitous decision, possibly even a manipulation on the part of our father, who had not yet been dead a day and was obviously still quite attached to his accomplishments. But it was in this manner that Eve came to her true vocation. Thirty years later, past the age our father was at his death, past typical retirement age, she is still the publisher and editor, and she has become something of an elder stateswoman in what is now very much "her" field.

Eve did not tell me about this contact until after I began writing this book. Even then she seemed concerned I might feel wounded. But this contact serves to illustrate the wisdom of the dead, for the work did not suit me. She and

I partnered in this endeavor for a few years until my own dreams called me to use my inheritance to return to school and earn my MA in interdisciplinary consciousness studies, a vibrant and exhilarating choice. My father had known, even before I did, that his magazine would not be a permanent career for me.

∾

Many of us are challenged to unearth the work that makes us sing. The dead, who exist in Spirit's clear light, sometimes give us a helping hand. Even coming to the cusp of death, which Susan Varon did only briefly following a major stroke, can accomplish this. It helped her move from "just living" as an administrative assistant to her true calling as an interfaith minister. Despite the numerous losses that this event brought her, she says she can only describe her stroke as "an unmixed blessing."

∾

Sarah was a successful Los Angeles fashion designer. She also had a certain knack for "knowing" outside the standard means, but it was casual, not a skill she focused on. One night she got up to go to the bathroom where she found one of her fashion models, Melody, in a vision sitting on the tub. With no preamble Melody said, I did a stupid thing by getting in the car with that photographer. She appeared to be mad at herself for not following her intuition. Sarah was totally mystified. She had had a few visitations from the dead before, but Melody was not dead. What could this vision mean?

The next day she learned that Melody had disappeared. The television news showed photos of the beautiful young woman. Her car had been found. A massive search was already in progress. Sarah didn't know what to do. No one knew whether Melody was dead or alive. It was abhorrent to Sarah to imagine being on Fox News with what might just be some odd hunch; she did nothing. Melody visited again, asking Sarah to tell her parents she was dead. *Okay,* Sarah thought, *if this is really Melody and Melody's really dead, and I'm so psychic, let's test this out.* "Tell me where your parents live," she demanded. Melody simply returned to berating herself for getting in a stranger's car for a "model interview." Sarah continued, albeit now even more uneasily, to do nothing.

The third time Melody visited, she arrived like a hurricane, yelling, They are going to find my body this afternoon! You have got to tell my parents I left my body right away when he ran over me. I died then. I was already dead when he did all those other things. I did not suffer, because I had already gone to the light. She repeated, still more forcefully, They are going to find my body this afternoon! Sarah's mission was now clear. She related all this to Melody's closest friend and got her, since she knew Melody's parents, to deliver the message before their daughter's body was found. Though I can barely imagine how horrible this was to hear, at least this message prevented them from thinking their daughter had experienced the strangling and other "obscene things" this man had done to her already-dead body. Sarah chose not to be specific about those things, and I did not press the point. Melody's obvious compassion for her parents, her ability to foresee the future—They are going to find my body this afternoon, which is exactly what happened—and her ability to find Sarah, who could see and hear her and act on what she heard, were a miraculous blessing for Melody's family and friends.

In addition, Sarah was encouraged to trust that what she can see and know that others cannot are more than idle hunches and can be of great value. She no longer lives in Los Angeles, no longer focuses her work on the fashion industry. She has trained and developed her innate psychic abilities and, through her vast experience, was full of information for me on connecting with the dead.

✍

Ted Wiard is a grief counselor, who founded and runs the Golden Willow Retreat Center in Arroyo Seco, New Mexico, with its Capillita de las Angelitas (Little Chapel of Little Angels), every beam and adobe brick graced with healing intention. The center provides sanctuary and support for anyone experiencing grief and loss. He writes a column on the subject for the *Taos News*, and Ted knows whereof he speaks. He came to this knowledge at great cost.

As a young man he was hospitalized with a parasite so forceful he had lost thirty-five pounds in four days. Out of nowhere he heard a voice say, In the morning you will either be dead or you will start getting better. He fell asleep relaxing into either possibility, and in the morning he began to get better. Who this disembodied voice belonged to and why it had come to him, he did not know, but he had trusted it. Now he credits this voice with being his first deep awareness of invisible support, the "first level of the scaffolding" that would later sustain him through the deaths of five beloveds.

Within a year, Ted's twenty-two-year-old brother Richard accidentally drowned. As Ted looks back, he can detect another touch of that invisible support, because during the week prior to Richard's death, his brother had visited numerous family members, made a deliberate connection with each one, and cemented it by giving them each a geode from his collection. The night before he drowned he had called Ted and said, out of the blue, "Don't forget now, I love you," not the most typical behavior for such a young man.

Days later, as Ted was driving, he cried out an ultimatum for a visible sign of Richard's continued existence. Phenomena began to occur. A huge elk appeared on the road, a particularly vivid rainbow arced in front of him. Ted responded angrily to each incident, "That's not big enough!" About a month later he awakened in the night to someone sitting on the edge of his bed. Instinctively, he kicked out hard, his foot going right through the body as though there were no one there. It was then he saw that this was his brother, smiling and radiating a quality of total love and warmth. After a shared moment of silence, his brother rose, silently admonished, Come on, Ted, enjoy, and walked through the bedroom wall. "That," Ted thought, "is big enough." Ted told me he is still often aware of his brother's energy.

Next, Ted's wife, the mother of their two young daughters, contracted cancer, and after a time she too passed away. Later, though it is almost too much to believe, his mother-in-law and both his daughters were killed together in a car accident. Within five years, his entire world imploded. Only too aware of the dichotomy, he raged at the same God whose existence he questioned. The enormity of his sorrow and rage filled his next few years. One day at a time, one emotion and thought at a time, one visitation at a time, his pain was transmuted into his calling. His wife visited in a vision with the same smile of unconditional love he had received from his brother. His daughters visit him too, though not with that kind of smile. Ted thinks this is because unconditional love is a given from children, they have no need to emphasize it. One daughter comes as the wiggle worm against his chest she had always been; the other comes calm and steady like her mother, lacing her fingers through his, her palm on the back of his hand as she used to do as he drove her to school. The presence and love and support of his dead beloveds have helped him go beyond surviving to thriving. Not that he told me any one of them said to do this or to do that, but their presence helped to heal him and then to awaken the parts of him necessary for the challenges of his new work.

Ted experienced his losses young. There were so many they emptied him out like the shaman who becomes a hollow reed, a conduit through which Spirit can move. He views his work as the equivalent of adding another step to a twelve-step program. It is the final creative step in our healing in which we offer what we've gleaned from our suffering back to the world. This final step is an essential aspect of returning to wholeness. We are so raw when we grieve that we may retreat from the world to lick our wounds like injured animals. Giving back binds us to the world and its beings once again. Some do this through making art or teaching or writing or by founding, leading, or speaking to bereavement groups, others through their music. Most give back in their daily lives through the compassion that can be heard in their voices, seen in their eyes and in the expressions on their faces.

ℰ☙

My friend Morten worded his inquiry about the value of contact with our dead beloveds this way: "To what end?" Those three simple words—"To what end?"—asked of our dreams, our intuitions, our daily lives and relationships, of our struggles, of our visions and visitations, have the potential to transform us all into shamans and wise ones, into seers and visionaries, people who live within the grace of a constantly increasing awareness. By keeping such a question alive as we grieve, after-death contact may fill in missing puzzle pieces.

At age eight, Keith's daughter died in a car accident, returning to him in dreams over the course of several years. She began by telling him it had been her time to go and that her death was no one's fault. Her mother had been driving; a moment of distraction as she picked up something her daughter had dropped had been the "cause" of the accident, so this no-fault statement made an important distinction. Later Keith's daughter explained in a dream how her death had been designed to assist her mother in working through a deeply embedded pattern. Keith called this a "soul contract." He was the only person—besides Randi—to use that phrase with me.

Certainly Kara did not call her husband's accidental death at age sixty-three part of their "contract," yet in retrospect she can see in it a sense of right order that began six months prior to the accident. In a talk at his college reunion he had advised that we prepare to leave this life with no regrets by making amends *now* with anyone with whom we have issues. He then proceeded to make those amends in his own life. After the car accident, in which Kara was also severely injured, she heard a voice say, Everything is working out, though we are not driving the bus. She did not know if this was her husband speaking. Kara told me she loved him deeply and misses him very much, yet she can see value in being without him now. "He was a powerhouse of a man. I tended to follow along in his wake." Now she is having the opportunity "to learn to be whole without him." Recently I saw a listing for a one-woman show of her paintings. I would say she's doing an excellent job of learning to be whole without him.

The word "contract" might apply to Jillis' story too. It brings the subject of reincarnation into the after-death contact conversation once more. From childhood on, her relationship with her alcoholic father had been an ongoing battle. Now, having been warned he might die before she got to the hospital, she was still ten minutes away when she suddenly saw him on the "inner screen" of her mind's eye. Internally, she reached out to grasp his hands in hers, saying silently, "You can have no more of me, but you can have all of this," as she transferred his hands from hers into the hands of the Mahanta—what members of Eckankar call the representative of the Divine. On her arrival, the nurses said her father had died exactly ten minutes earlier, just as she had offered him to Spirit. She asked to be alone with him. She placed her hand on his leg. "Old man," she began, and was immediately transported to a battle scene in another life in which she herself was a man, dressed in a pleated leather skirt and standing beside a charnel heap of dead soldiers. She became aware that in that lifetime, she and her father were commanders of opposing armies. In this scene, she had come to confirm that her "worthy opponent" was really dead. His body lay on top of the heap.

That word "worthy" is the keystone to the changes that occurred between them during the final part of her father's life. As she had let go of her expectations of him, her hatred had gradually let up. Now, looking back at his death, she asked large questions: What if he had waited to die until she was capable of offering him to Spirit at the moment of death? What if his suffering (I wonder if she includes her own here, too) was actually a gift? In other words, what if her father was still a "worthy opponent," not the abominable enemy she had so long considered him to be?

༄

Bobbi's experience covered many years from the time her husband Lou had been killed by a car when Bobbi was only twenty-two. Hindsight reveals fore-signs: A few days prior to the accident Lou had become convinced he would never see his grandfather again, though a Thanksgiving trip was planned for later that same week. Lou had been right. A few days after his death, a dear friend received a letter from him—which was decidedly odd, since he lived nearby and they saw one another frequently. Lou had enclosed a poem and across the top of it he had written, "In case I don't see you again." Then Bobbi found a Christmas gift under their bed, purchased and wrapped more than a month early, labeled, "To Bobbi, Love, Lou."

Eventually, though her hair turned permanently white beside Lou's deathbed, Bobbi Rapozo fell in love with and married Bill Cogger. Bill accepted her nightmares of Lou's death, that she still visited his grave and still wanted to be buried beside him in the plot she had purchased after his death. This plot was for Lou and for herself and for Lou's parents, who had become her surrogate parents.

Later, pregnant with Bill's child, she had a vision of Lou so real she was briefly positive he was alive and thoroughly confused over what on earth she would do about having two husbands. Lou spoke, lightly at first, before moving on to his true purpose. Everything up until now, he told her, falling in love with Bill and marrying, she was doing for the second time, but this baby was the beginning of a new life. You have to let me go now. I will see you again. This visitation helped her to move forward, though she still clung tightly to being buried beside Lou. Bobbi and Bill had children and grandchildren. They remained so close to Lou's parents that their children called them Grandma and Grandpa. "I loved Bill Cogger dearly," she told me, but after thirty-eight years he ended their marriage. When Bobbi went to inquire about Social Security benefits, she was amazed to discover that at age fifty-nine she had become eligible for a widow's pension from Lou. In 1970 she had been told there were no such benefits available. Now Lou's pension was much higher than what she would have gotten from either Bill's Social Security or her own.

She says she and Lou "have come full circle." They began together; he supports her now; they will be buried together. Equally important, she has maintained a close relationship with his parents for both herself and for her children. Our interview was delayed a week because of her annual Mother's Day trip to visit with ninety-four-year-old Mom Rapozo. Bobbi told me that when she married Lou she thought of him as a gift. When he died, she wondered why that gift had been given to her only to be taken away. "Now," she says, "I think he was the bearer of the gift. If you live long enough, you can begin to understand, to make some sense of what happens. If Lou was meant to die, at least I got his parents. In a way, I feel that Lou never left me."

"Use my whole name," she declared emphatically, when I asked. Roberta Rapozo Cogger is shorthand for her whole tale.

☙

This brings me now to the balance of my own "To what end?" story. Of course, I was comforted by the months of daily conversations with Randi. My grasp of how existence continues after death is still frequently reinforced by awareness of her subtle presence and support. But, like Jillis and her father, Randi and I have a history that precedes our current roles as mother and daughter. For me the concept of reincarnation resolved a dilemma that had long befuddled me.

I recall my childhood confusion over life's contrasts and extremes, like the difference between Beanie, our town's drooling, fifty-year-old errand "boy," his eager voice high-pitched as a child's, and Einstein with his genius; the gulf between Elizabeth Taylor's beautiful violet eyes and a deformed infant abandoned on church steps. I could not fathom how innocent prisoners could spend years on death row, only to be released; how soldiers, mere boys, could return from war for their own funerals; or how the Rockefellers could have so much power and wealth. Out of these contradictions arose my large questions. Somehow, despite my family's agnosticism, I knew there was a God. I was certain that this God was one of grace and love, not the scowling, bearded old white man, complete with his own lightning bolt, I saw framed on my girlfriend's wall. I was certain "my" God was generous and kind. I still thought of God back then as a he, not the more than he and she that I perceive this force to be now. I was equally certain there had to be a way to make sense of those extremes of experience I was observing. I was also sure no one was being punished or rewarded. I even knew that if there were earthly rewards, wealth and beauty might not be among them.

When I was in my early twenties, my husband came home with a book by a Tibetan monk named Lobsang Rampa, and reincarnation and karma entered my world. It was a revelation to realize we experience it all. We are born again and again and again, male and female, starving or obese, famous, rich, or poor, we die young or at one hundred. In this manner, over many lifetimes, we learn the deep compassion and wisdom that is the result of walking in another's shoes. Karma is not punishment, rather it is life offering us the opportunity to learn and grow. If the tyrant is later reborn as a slave, it is not because he or she was "bad," but to experience how difficult it is to be powerless. We are reborn and reborn until we learn to respect life and not to kill, to be generous and not to steal, to be loyal and not to betray. We walk in many shoes until our wholeness and love and wisdom are perfect reflections of the godhead, until we align with that which is eternal—call it soul, spirit, consciousness—the part of us that never dies.

More recently, questions have arisen about time. These have muddied my concept of life after life after life. Over much of my adulthood, usually once every decade or so, awareness of another lifetime has come to me spontaneously, sometimes in meditation, sometimes in dreams, sometimes during ordinary, waking consciousness. Each new life has illuminated and helped me to resolve some issue in my current life. I have always called these recalls "past" lives, but are they really past? If the sacred reality is timeless, how do these lives nest together? Am I recalling the past or is this the only means my human mind has to contain other lives? Could these lives all be happening right now? And if so, how can that be? Philosophers of science endlessly debate the question, "What is time?" My thoughts are suppositions and my mind dances awkwardly with the timeless state. Theoretical explanations seem too logical for my vast mind, not logical enough for my ordinary one. I am left within the poetic riddle of not fully understanding.

Still, I know my daughter Randi and I have experienced alternate lives together beyond (perhaps before) our current one. I now recognize that our current experience, with all of its suffering, has done much to heal our other times together. I am no fatalist. I do not see life as set on a predetermined course by some external energy. We have free will, yet there is a momentum to the river that winds its way toward wholeness. Among the infinite options available to us, if we come to the banks of that river, we may be blessed to discover aspects of the transcendent design of our lives.

I have long trusted that a divine pattern underlies my life, and I have sought to understand it. When my daughter died, I saw nothing divine in her death. I was conscious only of finding a way to be with it. I heard about the need to accept it; I could not. I was urged to "find closure" with it: anathema. Why would I want to close Randi out? I attended an all-day event for those who have had a beloved die by suicide. A mother spoke of the choice she had had to maintain connection with her dead son either through grief or through love. She chose love, although letting go of her grief was terrifying at first. It left her rudderless for the moment it took to reclaim their love connection. Love is what I will choose, I thought, though at two months out I was not yet ready to release my grief.

My friend Kate's daughter had been murdered. She and I decided that our goal was to make peace with these deaths. Eventually we discarded that aim too in order to learn how to be present with our losses. The path to this goal was challenging. I stumbled forward through the boulders of my pain. When my daughter responded to my keening with, Mom, we *contracted* for this, her words jammed broken glass into my wounds. Contracts smacked of courts and laws. Even if she were right, I did not think I could ever say the word "contract" out loud, or even here on paper. I could barely stand to think of having "contracted" for my daughter's death. I noted the quotes I had long ago placed on my altar. From one of my teachers: "Accept every moment as if you had chosen it. This will miraculously transform your life." A prayer, by poet Galway Kinnell, about wanting what is. [2] I had been drawn to these words before the depth of this loss had touched me. Now I did not know how to apply them.

I read and I pondered and I prayed and I pondered and I prayed and I read. Abstract theories, possible answers, came from my reading. From Michael Newton's work with the period *between* the lives of his clients, I read about groups of souls gathering to create intentions for their upcoming lives that would serve as goals other than our human desire not to suffer. Randi used that dreaded word "contract" more than once. I don't recall if I asked her what she meant. Maybe the word disturbed me so much I did not, or maybe I did and she did not reply. Sometimes our exchanges were Zen koans; I was left on my own to determine their meaning. I could not see how such a contract could serve us or the good of the whole, how a divine design could cause such pain for so many. Besides her family and her friends, she had brought so many babies into this world. What must the mothers of those babies feel?

When Randi had been in her early twenties and we were in nearly constant disagreement, I had asked—in meditation—to be shown why. I saw a lifetime in which she was my mistress and I her slave. This new information helped me, and then us, after I shared it with her, to love another a little more gracefully.

In another meditation, I had seen another alternate life, though I detected no connection with Randi. In that life I was an indigenous Mexican mother with babe in arms. It was the early 1500s. Mexico was being invaded by the Spanish. A conquistador thrust himself upon me, knocking my baby daughter to the ground. When he had finished, he stabbed me and left me to die. My baby sobbed out of reach. She was too young to crawl to me, and I was too wounded to go to her. I prayed that she not be harmed. I prayed that she not be hurt. In desperation I prayed that I would rather she die than to be hurt in any way. As I said those last words, another conquistador came by, took the scene in at a glance, drew his sword, and slit my naked girl baby from vulva to chin. She died instantly while I lingered on.

As I lay dying, I had an eon to regret my prayers, to decide I was a despicable mother who prayed despicable prayers to a God who was despicable enough to answer them. Thus began thirty lifetimes in which I died too young to have children, or my children died young or, as in my lifetime as a slave, they were taken from me. Not for me those romantic past-life recalls as Marie Antoinette or Cleopatra, someone exotic and famous. When I processed that Mexican life, I thought it explained why, in a family where college was a given, I had dropped out and become a mother twice over before turning twenty-two. I came to think that mothering and learning once again to open to the sacred, to pray, and to believe in my right to parenthood, were the overriding purposes of this lifetime. With an amount of hubris that now embarrasses me, I thought I had done a damned good job of achieving my purpose in being born this time around. Then my daughter Randi took her own life. My fine ideas crashed in a heap. When enough time had passed, I noted how that Mexican experience reminded me not to take responsibility for Randi's death, not to be devoured by that twin legacy of suicide—guilt and blame. By now the pieces of the puzzle of our lives together were spread out in front of me, but the blue pieces of the sky and the sea looked identical. I could not complete the picture. This is where Randi's after-death wisdom and support with two of my dreams became indispensible.

I'll start with the second dream, which I had when Randi had been dead for a year. This dream contained the enigmatic phrase, "the value of a valuable bird even when dead," which kept niggling at me to remember the details of an earlier dream about a bird. That dream was a vague blur. I had no idea when I'd had it, but I was determined to find it. I set aside a morning, made myself a cup of tea, and at random pulled out a dozen of my dream notebooks. At random I selected one about two years old and settled in to start my search. Within five minutes I was reading the prior bird dream. To my astonishment I saw I had dreamed it the night

Randi had made what we call her "big attempt" and Chelsey had found her unconscious in the morning. Perhaps Randi had been taking those pills as I dreamed. In my dream, I find a tiny dead bird inside my house. I tenderly nestle this vibrant yellow, orange, royal blue, scarlet, and bright green bird into a handled basket of lingerie on my dresser. When I return later, the bird comes to life in my hand and struggles to fly away. I fall in love with it, and it responds to my caress. I offer the luscious tame little bird to Randi as the Supreme Gift, which is how I had titled the dream, "The Supreme Gift."

The delight with which I had awakened from this dream quickly veered into hell. When we received the phone call that Randi was in the hospital, the dream was all but forgotten. Now, with both dreams in front of me, I knew they formed a whole, but I still did not know how. As I surveyed them both, Randi visited, and together we explored them. What emerged were at least some answers to questions like, "To what end had I lived those thirty lifetimes?" and "To what end were we mother and daughter." She told me she had been my infant daughter in that Mexican lifetime and that we had come full circle. In both lifetimes, though the circumstances were quite different, I, as her mother, had made an opening for death to occur. I find it essential to emphasize that those are Randi's words. When I offered her the gift of that bird in my dream, she told me now, You gave me permission to die. This was the greatest gift you could have given me, and the hardest. Only a mother can know at what cost. This was like being asked to swallow that broken glass. Randi said that how I had reacted to her death in this lifetime—without self-blame—is the healing of how, in that alternate lifetime, I had taken on her death as if I had drawn the sword myself. She said it was time for me to understand that the fact that I could, if only symbolically in my dreams, see the depth of her suffering and allow her to die, was a Supreme Gift. She said she had come to me from the threshold of death in the sacred reality of the dream world, and I had gifted her with this beautiful bird to lift her out of her suffering. She said that in our Mexican lifetime I had also known that her suffering, had she lived, would have been too great to bear.

We did not speak of our mistress and slave lifetime, but the love we were experiencing erased those former struggles as though they had never been. I found an exchange in my "Randi Messages" notebook from before this in which she had said, I want to heal the rift between us. I had asked if that included ones beyond this current lifetime. I speak only of the totality had been her reply.

This tale is written from the center of my personal universe and illuminates only a tiny element of what must surely be an intricate mandala. Surely Randi did not simply sacrifice her life on the altar of mine if, to the soul, death is even considered a sacrifice. So many questions remain. Did this contract, or sacred covenant as I prefer to think of it, require that she die in the prime of life when her daughter was only eighteen? Did it require that she die by suicide? What discoveries remain for her? What is she learning now about her choices? What about the effect of her death on her daughter? Could she have chosen a different manner and time to die and still served the original intentions? What has this experience brought her sister and father and stepparents and friends and other relatives and coworkers? What are their "To what end?" stories? Have they too had alternate lives together? What others will we all experience? What is it I have not yet seen and have yet to learn?

Perhaps after my own death, there will be more answers. It seems a great privilege to have touched at least a toe on solid ground beneath the quicksand of my daughter's death. This toehold has been an enlightening experience. Still I remain standing in the midst of the unknown.

Chapter Nine

ONE LIFE, ABRIDGED

Suffering opens the heart.
It is its gift.

— *Randi Galavitz White,*
After-death communication, May 27, 2011

You have just read the panoramic overview of my relationship with my daughter, and how her guidance and wisdom
helped to restore me after her death. This is the pretty version of the tale, but there is also what brought us to the
moment of her suicide. The memory of the day Randi was
found dead has been carved into my bones as if into a marble
tombstone. For the first time since then I find myself able to
write about it and what led to it. This is an essential element
of our story, because it is the intensity of how the trauma
shredded my heart that opened me to receive my daughter's
visitations.

From the start, life challenged Randi; often it challenged
me to be her mother. As an infant, she was colicky: she cried,

slept erratically, was acutely sensitive to sound. As a child, she was excessively sensitive to others' criticisms and moods and feelings. To her credit, if she burst in from playing to make a simple request—"Can I go to Billy's after lunch?"—and my face revealed any hint of moodiness, she'd wait, ask me later. To her detriment, a teacher's incorrect accusation for a small infraction caused her torrents of suffering. At Randi's memorial service a midwife described the gentle way Randi had talked her through her grief and angst following a birth in which the baby had died. This woman had been ready to give up her work until Randi helped her to remember its joyful parts. "But I believe Randi was too tender for this world," she said.

When Randi was thirteen, her jaw was shattered by a kick from her own horse, as if—the surgeon explained—it were a seashell placed on concrete and smashed by a sledgehammer. He mended the jaw, but it was irreparably damaged. A few years later, another beloved horse of hers was injured and did not survive. This loss seemed to irreparably damage her psyche. Over the next decades there were many jaw surgeries; she learned to live with constant pain. There were also elective plastic surgeries, breast reductions, a nose job, lip work, hip work. Underlying this was a difficulty with relationships and a tendency to isolate. She always had trouble sleeping, exacerbated by her profession, which entailed interrupted nights on call.

Her daughter was seventeen when the final, brutal chapter of Randi's life began, with threats of suicide, bouts of tears, a deep, deep depression, and suicide attempts. We—her family, the women's clinic where she worked, the Colorado medical oversight folks—all urged or, in professional cases, required various kinds of help: psychiatry, psychotherapy, medications, and residential programs. Just once I got her to talk on the phone with a woman from such a program. When Randi asked whether they would allow her to take her pain meds, she was told they would help her to get off them. She did not let the conversation continue much beyond that and refused to consider their program. Apparently, to Randi, life without her pain meds was impossible.

I had long worried that she was addicted to these. For decades the medical profession was cautious about addictions and had refused to prescribe opioids for chronic pain. She first encountered opioids at about the time the medical profession began to prescribe them more freely. Now it appears that changed approach was a mistake. Information is emerging about the problems of long-term use. Many people with chronic pain have become addicted to their painkillers, many have turned from prescribed to illegal drugs, and many have died. I am convinced addiction to her prescribed medications played a significant role in my daughter's difficulties.

❧

One evening Chelsey called to say her mom was making suicide threats. As we were assessing what to do, I asked, "What's happening right now?"

"She's cleaning up the kitchen." This made no sense; five minutes earlier she'd been saying she wanted to die.

"She's cleaning up the kitchen?"

"She's mumbling she doesn't want it to be messy when the EMTs come for her in the morning."

"Hang up and call 911," I said. She was clever, my Randi. Very late that night a hospital social worker told her, "I know you're manipulating me," but he still let her go home. Looking back, I wonder how it is I know that's what he said. Did she tell Chelsey and then Chelsey told me? Was Randi proud of her ability to talk herself out of the hospital's clutches? Why else would she share this?

∽

I was horrified when Spencer and I arrived at Randi's house one Friday and she privately told me she had made a failed attempt to die by overdose the night before. "I just overslept and went to work," she said with a maddening equanimity. The next day she had a seizure. She'd had seizures before, and after she recovered, the EMTs were prepping to leave. I told them of her attempt and insisted they take her to the hospital in case there was some connection to the drug overdose. Really what I meant was, in case they could—please, dear God—help her somehow. She was required by law to spend three days in a psychiatric hospital because of her attempt. We were allowed to visit her for one specific hour each day. I thought my knees would buckle as we went through their security screening to be sure we did not bring her contraband drugs or weapons.

We visited in a well-guarded room full of other patients. Some looked quite ordinary; others seemed dazed or angry or isolated themselves in corners. Spencer and I were granted a brief meeting with a staff therapist who cautiously hinted that borderline personality disorder might be an issue. Maybe she wasn't permitted to formally diagnose? Was that the psychiatrists' task? I think we asked her a lot of questions, though I can't recall her answers. I was almost as dazed as the patients in that group room. Did we ask to talk with the psychiatrist? I can't remember that either. I bought the book on borderline personality disorder the therapist recommended and read it within a day. Randi fit the profile, though what good a name for her condition was, I did not know. Later, Randi wouldn't discuss it and wasn't interested in the book. She only said her psychiatrist had given her medication for "poor impulse control," one of the symptoms. It was just more drugs to add to the soup of her pain meds, her sleeping meds, her antidepressants.

My insistence that the EMTs take her to the hospital was monumental, because it exposed her suicidal state within the medical community. She lost her hospital privileges, and she was livid. She wouldn't accept my phone calls. She wouldn't allow me to visit. I called suicide helplines and mental health associations. I found out how hard it is to get a functioning adult committed. I was powerless to help. I went into therapy. I felt terrified. The ringing of the phone made my entire body clench. Spencer and I had the worst fight of our twenty-plus years together. Chelsey kept in touch, but she vacillated between openness and anger—sometimes at her mother, sometimes at me—afraid, no doubt, that I would take her mother away, that her mother would die, that her mother was crazy. She must have been just terrified,

I imagine, as I was, of what the next moment or the next morning might bring.

യ

When Randi finally regained consciousness after her "big attempt," in a hoarse whisper she hurled her first words like darts: "Mom, don't you dare tell them anything." This time her attempt was no secret. I had nothing to tell anyone that wasn't already known. I only stayed in Colorado with her for a couple of weeks. Randi accepted my presence at first, but she was unequivocal about when it was time for me to leave. Still, the year between that big attempt and her death held occasional moments of joy. Chelsey's high school graduation was a sweet time full of visiting family, love, and pride. It was obvious Randi was glad to be alive for this occasion. There was an afternoon at her favorite place, the waterfall in Manitou Springs, with her blond dog Angel romping in the water. Within the year we would scatter Randi's ashes in that waterfall.

യ

That final week, when Chelsey came home from college on Thursday afternoon and couldn't wake her mother up, Randi convinced yet another hospital social worker that the overdose had been accidental: she'd been unable to sleep, just taken too much medication in the night. She convinced Chelsey the overdose was an accident. On the phone, she convinced me, too. Chelsey sounded so playful when she told me about wearing her mom's scrubs to the hospital and what fun it was to pretend to be a doctor. On Sunday, once Randi was stable, they released her, and Chelsey drove her mom home, tucked her in, and left for her dorm, promising to return on Thursday.

When Randi and I talked on the phone later that evening, for the umpteenth time I offered to come. I was learning to follow her lead, not to push my presence on her. "You don't need to, Mom. You're coming next week. I'm okay." Next week I was to drive her to Denver for an appointment with a pain specialist for a procedure of some sort, something new—neither drugs nor surgery—to help with the pain. I would have to cancel that appointment a few days later.

"I'm okay, Mom, really," Randi reassured me again.

"I'll call you in the morning," I promised.

"No, Mom, don't call. I'll probably sleep in. I'm okay, but I'm tired. I'll call you later. And Mom, Chelsey and I are coming to New Mexico for Thanksgiving. You can count on us. We talked it over in the hospital." She was her old self; that sweet lilt she used to have was back in her voice. I relaxed. It had been an accident, not an attempt. Though I wondered, could she keep on living alone with her judgment so impaired? That we would have to deal with later. In the meantime I would plan our Thanksgiving menu. For Randi and Chelsey, we had to have both sweet potatoes and mashed potatoes. That was a given.

☙

On Monday I awoke with a mild recurrence of my old case of shingles. I waited all day for a call from Randi, not allowing myself to call her. She had asked me not to and said *she* would call me. I had to learn to trust her; I had to learn to discipline my fears. She often did not answer her phone. If I called and she didn't pick up, terror drained the blood from my head. I did not call. I could not panic every time she didn't reach out or didn't pick up.

On Tuesday the shingles were worse. And Randi still hadn't called. By the afternoon I surrendered. I called her exactly when I knew she'd be getting ready for her one o'clock doctor's appointment. She did not pick up. "Dammit to hell, Randi, don't you know how I worry?" This was my cover for fear. She did not pick up after the appointment either. On Wednesday I awoke with a full-blown shingles outbreak, something that had not happened since the first time, and I left early for the eight o'clock walk-in clinic. I went to the pharmacy to fill my prescription. I allowed myself to run a single errand. I called her when I got home. She did not pick up.

⁊

At that precise moment the final countdown began. At each stage of it, I left messages and had lengthy waits for replies. I paced and I prayed—pleaded is more like it. I was not functional. Spencer's face was a mask of worry. I could not bear to be more than one step away from the phone. When Chelsey finally returned my call, I leapt at it like a hungry tiger before the first ring was through. We chatted, oh-so-casually, about her college classes. She was eager to be going home the next day, excited that she and her mom were getting along so well. When I thought we'd talked long enough not to awaken Chelsey's suspicions, I slipped in my question, still managing to keep my tone oh-so-casual: "Have you talked to your mom?"

"No, she's not picking up."

CHING.

I left a message for Randi's doctor. He and the office staff knew of her prior attempts. "Have you seen Dr. White? This is her mother." It took an eon for anyone to call me back.

"No, Dr. White missed her appointment and hasn't returned our calls. We're worried, too. It's not like her. She's so responsible."

CHING. CHING.

I called her friend Judi at work at the women's clinic and had another interminable wait for her reply. "Have you talked to Randi?"

"No, she's not picking up."

CHING. CHING. CHING.

Judi and I made a plan. She would go to the house at five when she got off work. I was astounded to see that it was nearly five already. She had a key, but if Randi did not answer the door, Judi said she would not go in. She knew. We talked about it later. We all knew. Judi, Chelsey, me—we all knew. Spencer was scared, but he wouldn't let himself be sure. Now I think the shingles were my body's reaction to Randi pulling on me from the other side of death to prevent Chelsey from coming home to her three-day-dead body. While I was trying to train myself not to panic at an unanswered phone, not to bug my daughter too much, my body knew. My nervous system knew. The shingles-damaged nerves always reacted to stress. This was stress as serious as it comes.

Judi and I decided I would call the police department for a "well-check." Judi would wait in her car for their arrival, unless, by some miracle, Randi answered the door. I told the woman who answered the phone Randi's history and my fears. I was almost as terrified of Randi's fury at me if she were just "not picking up" as I was terrified of what the police might find. "Emergencies come first, so it might be a while," the woman said gently. She asked if there were guns in the house or animals. "The dog, Angel, is small and sweet; Shiloh, the cat, can be nasty but will hide," I said. "There are no guns."

Randi did not answer the door. Judi sat out front, giving me blow-by-blow reports. The garage door gaped open, which was not right. She could hear Angel barking inside the house. A police car arrived with a single policewoman. She assessed the situation and refused to enter the house alone. She called for support and went to talk with the neighbors. No one could say how long the garage door had been open. Had Randi left it that way to alert a neighbor to find her? The neighbors gawked in groups on the sidewalk and on the cul-de-sac, whispering together. When the second police car arrived, the two officers entered the house through the unlocked inside garage door.

After an age, the ambulance came. The EMTs hurried in. When they walked back out again, they were no longer in a rush. The ambulance left with its gurney empty. "I know what that means," Judi told me. "The coroner will come next." I knew. We knew. Yet we didn't. You can't know such a thing. You can't really know your daughter is dead, or your friend. It's impossible to take in. I was still waiting for it to be a mistake. They would call the ambulance back, wouldn't they? Wouldn't they? It was just one more in this hideous series of failed attempts, wasn't it? I asked Judi to have the policewoman call me. Officer Ryan sounded young and scared, and it was obvious she was not allowed to tell me my daughter was dead. It must be that only coroners can do that. I found myself trying to comfort her, an odd reversal of roles, if ever there was one.

I was still waiting for it to be a mistake when the coroner's white van arrived. After what felt like hours, though surely it was only some minutes, the coroner called me. The coroner told me. The coroner did not sound young or scared. She sounded competent and caring. I was grateful that there had been no gruff, brusque male voices, that she too was a woman. I wondered if she was a mother and what this must be like for her. As we spoke, she fumbled a word or two, hesitating. I tensed. Why would she do that? What worse thing could she have to tell me? She explained that sometimes people worry about the animals, that they might have "done something." Done something? Done something? That was a worry I had not thought of. "They did not," she reassured me. I would not let my mind go too far into what Angel and Shiloh had not done.

When we arrived at Randi's house later, we would see that Officer Ryan or the coroner or both of them had cleaned up the dog poop and the litter box, put a dog-piss-soaked throw rug out in the garage, laid out fresh food and water for Angel and Shiloh. Every door was locked, and they had left lights on. On the phone, the coroner had expressed concern that the house would be empty. "The whole neighborhood knows," she told me. "We're coming tonight," I replied. "It's two hundred miles. We only have to pack." Woman-like, my mind flashed on the question: What should I pack for my daughter's funeral?

Judi skipped reporting when they carried Randi out to the white coroner's van. She told me when the van left. By law, the coroner had said, an autopsy was required to determine the cause of death. There were to be other rules. They would keep the original suicide note as evidence indefinitely, in case anyone ever raised the question of whether her death was a murder, not suicide. We would only ever receive a photocopy of it. I wanted the one with her DNA on it, flakes of her skin, the one she had touched. I don't know why, when it was so hellish to read, but it was ours and I was angry that they could keep it from us.

Judi and I made a plan for telling Chelsey, but it failed miserably. Judi and her husband Leonard would drive to the university. I would tell Chelsey about her mom on the phone while they were both there with her. Leonard would drive Chelsey's car, while Judi drove Chelsey in their car to their home. Everything got all messed up. Chelsey got a call from a worried friend whose mother could see the commotion at the house from a distance. Somehow in the course of talking with Chelsey about this, I got confused. I thought she meant that she had been told by her friend; I thought Chelsey knew her mother was dead. She didn't, so she found out from me by default, from my assumption that she knew. She found out as she sat on the floor outside her dorm room, surrounded by frightened eighteen-year-olds, while she waited for Judi and Leonard to drive the forty miles to hold her in their arms.

In between all this I left the worst phone message possible for our friend Olga, "Pick up! Pick up! We need you to come over. We think she's dead." I did not need to explain who "she" was. I called my friends Anna and Steve. They were with us in five minutes. How was I to call my daughter Rowena in Mexico City? If I called her cell phone—all she had—I might get her on the street. I could not tell her on the street. I could not leave an urgent message either. She'd know at once. We'd all been living on red alert for so long. If my message wasn't urgent, she might not call me back until tomorrow. Instead I called her friend. "Is it her sister?" was the first thing he asked. Red Alert. He went to Rowena's apartment so she and my grandson weren't alone when I told them.

I called Randi and Rowena's father in Florida. His wife answered the phone. "I need to talk to Bob."

"He can't come to the phone right now."

"This is really important. I have to talk to him."

"Is it Randi?"

"Yes. Let me talk to Bob."

"Is Randi dead?" Red Alert. I told myself to breathe, while I decided how to answer. I should tell Bob first, shouldn't I? After all, he was Randi's father.

"Yes," I said, and she began to scream. I laid the receiver on the counter, and we all stared at it until we heard Bob say hello.

I had promised Rowena I'd call her on arrival at Randi's. She was worried about us driving so long, so late, and in such a state. Randi's phone would not allow an out-of-country call. We had no cell phone. The phone card in my wallet had expired. We found ourselves at Walmart past midnight. People were buying clothes and candy bars and beer, smiling and talking loudly, even laughing. I felt I should go over to each one and gently, tenderly, so as not to shock them too much, let them know that Randi was dead. Obviously they didn't know or they would not have been going about such ordinary business.

How could they not know? The world had imploded, hadn't it?

ℰℐ

Of course, it had not. Only our own small world had imploded, shrapnel bursting inward to violently splinter hearts, opening mine wide to embrace not only my grief but the after-death contact that emerged from the open wound like a white healing flower.

Chapter Ten

PARTING THE VEIL BETWEEN THE LIVING AND THE DEAD

Linear time is stopped when the gates between the worlds are opened.
— *Robert Moss,* The Dreamer's Book of the Dead

Is it possible for the living to part the veil we sense hanging between us and our dear dead ones? Can we initiate or encourage an exchange through this veil or must we wait for the dead to lift the curtain? It's not usually effective to insist. Instead, we open ourselves and invite connection. We can, as when expecting any invited guest, sweep the front walk of debris, put on the porch light, unlock the door, and listen for a knock. We cannot guarantee our guests' arrival, but we can be ready for them if they come.

For many of us our spiritual and imaginal feet have been bound by our culture and upbringing. If we claimed as children to see what others did not, we were likely to be scolded with, "It's only your imagination." Yet "only" is a poor descriptor for the powerful tool of imagination that every artist, inventor, and visionary leader uses to pry open the window into new possibilities. Without imagination we are trapped in the limitations of the visible worlds. In her memoir, Yvette Melanson tells of her dying mother coming to her, when she was a girl, to say goodbye. She quotes the same words her father, and others, had heard her mother say aloud as she "imagined" Yvette was with her. Yet he cannot believe Yvette has heard this from a distance and calls her a liar.[1] This is how we may pass our own denial training down to our children.

I stand by the statement I made in my preface that this would not be a self-help book with a bulleted list of sure ways to make contact with our dead beloveds. The suggestions I will make in this chapter carry no guarantees, for we need to remember that who receives after-death communication, along with why, lies in the territory of the ineffable. Yet there are ways to make ourselves more available to the possibility of contact, and we can increase the odds of noticing our beloveds if they do visit us. These methods are not fixed though; we must each make our own way. Here I want to place a note of caution: If we are deep in the throes of grief, still in a constant state of yearning for our dead beloved to be alive, to turn to the following suggestions too soon may only add to our heartache. The dead know when contact will rile up our emotions, and they are likely to keep their distance to protect us from suffering. If we experiment with these methods and are not aware of contact, we could add disappointment to our grief. Please choose among my suggestions with care and self-compassion until the initial grief has eased.

℃৩

One element that can interfere with our awareness of contact is whether we can allow ourselves to imagine the possibility that even a small contact could be real. When I asked my daughter Randi why she did not visit her sister Rowena, she said, I do. She does not know I'm there. This refrain surfaces repeatedly in material channeled from the dead. The dead knock on our doors, but we don't open them. At a public event, my daughter Rowena noticed a woman who looked so much like her deceased sister, she gasped and tears rose. Because she "knew" this could not possibly be her sister, she did what many do: she briefly closed her eyes and shook her head to clear it of what she was sure was a visual trick. She did not know that this means of contact is so common it is called "doubling." Rowena is an accomplished visual artist—both a painter and a textile artist—so the visual was an obvious way for Randi to attempt to make her presence known.

We can choose to acknowledge with gratitude the possibility that we may have actually seen our grandpa or our sister, even if we're not positive. Wendy Jordan, the author and Reiki practitioner in chapter 8, detected her tendency with personal losses to be skeptical of subtle hints of contact. She describes this as a "response of the mind" like Rowena's very logical and sensible, "That can't be my sister." Wendy says she's learning to simply say thank you, suggesting that gratitude for one small contact is a response that encourages another. A thank-you softens the heart. It is like saying, "I would love to see you." Even if we are sure of a contact, often we want more than we receive. If we've had a kiss in a dream, we long for an embrace. If we've heard, "I'm okay," we yearn for a conversation. When we express gratitude, either in the presence of uncertainty or when we long for more contact, we participate in an exchange and open a space for a response.

ↄ

Respecting all of our dreams and writing them down can encourage contact through them and increase the likelihood of remembering an ADC dream. Many of us will never see a vision or hear a disembodied voice, but whether we have recall or not, we all do dream. While we are in this nighttime realm, it can expand awareness to pay attention to those moments just before and after sleep that bridge the waking and dreaming realms and mingle the levels of reality. It's not accidental that so many ADC visions and visits occur in the bedroom when our bodies are quiet and our minds slowed or slowing. By honoring this state we honor and welcome that which is more than the physical. There is an art more than a skill to the mystical. A painter may call it a loose wrist. A dancer might say he floats upward instead of leaps, as if he has released the string on a helium-filled balloon. Receiving after-death communication resembles such artistic endeavors; it asks us to listen and to allow.

I introduce the topic of psychics, or mediums or channels, with caution, because it seems contrary to my entire intention of illustrating the availability of making contact on our own. Yet for certain people a psychic can, as one woman puts it, "initiate the conversation." Like all the ideas I present, please only take action on this one if it resonates. Part of my hesitation is that if resonance is based on a belief that we cannot make contact directly, depending on the psychic selected, that belief could be strengthened. Certain psychics do see part of their purpose as getting clients to understand they don't need an intermediary, though even some of these prescribe what I view as unnecessarily lengthy and costly educational regimens. In considering a psychic, please seek out personal recommendations and ask questions up front. Inquire whether this person wants to help clients learn to make contact themselves and what that help might entail in time and in money.

That said, a hand up can sometimes reveal that contact is already happening. I gave my granddaughter Chelsey a single psychic session that did exactly that. She burst out of the room afterward joyously shouting, "Mom is happy! She visits us as hawks and eagles and butterflies. I see butterflies everywhere!"

"She visits us as hawks?" My memory reeled backward. My relationship with hawks as guides had preceded Randi's death by a few years and began as a practice in listening to nature. On the mornings of long driving trips, I would ask Hawk to let me know of any dangers ahead, a whiteout, say, on the 10,000-foot La Veta Pass. Over time Hawk and I had developed a practical way to communicate. After Randi's death the messages got even more clear. I thought this was because grief had opened my inner eyes and ears. On the most startling trip to her house in Colorado Springs, I had seen seventeen hawks in two hundred miles. Most of them were in what I call their "warning" position perched on a pole or a tree to my left, yet there were no problems on the road. Why seventeen hawks and why were they all on the left? My answer came on arrival at Randi's house, where a uniformed man worked a long tool down a hole in the driveway. Water gushed from the garage. Huge icicles dangled from its roof. There had been an unprecedented windchill factor of minus forty degrees overnight. Pipes had frozen and burst in hundreds of homes and apartments. Randi's furnace had frozen and failed. The house was uninhabitable for more than three months. Seventeen hawks had tried to prepare me.

The winter following Chelsey's psychic session, she was caught driving friends on a snowy highway with snarled traffic and fishtailing tractor-trailers. Chelsey was so focused on the road she noticed nothing else, so it was her friends who pointed out there were hawks everywhere. It was her friends who gasped as they told her an eagle had landed in a nearby tree, risen up, flapped its huge wings, and settled back down again. This showed Chelsey that her mother's protective energy was available in such a treacherous situation. During the emotional breakup with a boyfriend, though we had never seen them there before, hawks even began to appear in Chelsey's suburban neighborhood.

I still don't know when my hawk guidance switched to Randi-through-hawk guidance. My husband and friends have grown accustomed to the fact that if we stand talking outside, especially if the talk turns to spiritual matters or to Randi, a hawk will sometimes nearly graze the tops of our heads. With all the contact I had had with Randi, I would have scoffed at the very thought of a psychic session for myself, yet look what Chelsey's one session revealed to us both.

In very different ways, my interviewee Henry's psychic sessions were an immense support to both him and his young, dying wife, who could not talk, yet through the psychic did so nonstop. Among many other things, she told him she was "okay," just as the dead so often do. Because these contacts were pre-death, this illustrates once again how much comfort the grace that surrounds, and sometimes precedes, a death can bring.

Karen hoped to be able to make direct contact herself, so her psychic asked those who came into her session, including both her birth parents and her adoptive parents, if they could help her to be aware of their contact. Each person told of typical times and ways when they visited, including a beloved grandmother who said she left "patterns in the sand but no footprints." Karen says now she has subtle awareness of visitations and that the feeling is one of a strengthened love connection with all her family. She leads an exceedingly busy life and told me that she may "move too fast" to get more concrete awareness of contact, which is in itself a suggestion. To encourage contact, we need to slow down and give ourselves the time and space to notice it.

Making an arrangement, before death, to make contact afterward, as I did with my friend Anne in chapter 1, is one more way to increase the odds of receiving and recognizing contact. When Anne came exactly as she said she would, as a violet-green swallow, the level of comfort I felt at the specificity of her visitation eased and settled me by making it blatantly clear that her consciousness had continued. You read of Rosalie's less specific approach in chapter 7. She simply asked her dying husband if he would be her guardian angel. He replied that he would if he could, and after his death he visited repeatedly.

We need not wait until death is imminent. We could arrange right now with our closest beloved—or the closest one who would not dismiss the idea as foolish—for how we would visit one another when we die. We could go through this book together looking for ideas that interest us. Do we have personal jokes or favorite puns? Are our strengths verbal, visual, tactile? Do we have a strong connection with nature or with our dreams? What if we were to make a plan, write it down, and store it with our wills and other end-of-life documents? This would create an alert stance in which we would be more attuned to watching for and recognizing contact. Making the plan could aid us to remember that in every lasting love story—whether between husband and wife, parent and child, friend and friend—beloveds enter into a bond that will in time be altered by the physical death of one or the other.

❧

Even something as pragmatic as writing our wills helps us to acknowledge death's reality, at least on a mental level. On the shelf opposite me I can see my copy of Virginia Morris' book, *Talking about Death Won't Kill You*. Often we act as though even thinking about death would jinx us. A seventy-two-year-old man is diagnosed with Stage IV cancer. His next five years are packed with surgeries, experimental procedures, chemotherapy, and radiation. Three weeks before he dies, he writes his will. Did he imagine he could trick death into passing him by, if he pretended it would never happen to him? How was it for his wife and family that he never once admitted aloud that he might die of this disease until days before he did?

Acknowledging that illness may come, and death will too—possibly when we least expect it—we can prepare now. We can write an advance directive, a power of attorney, or a Five Wishes document[2] to address our values around decisions about being put on artificial life support. These are tremendously loving actions, because the burden of undone and disorganized paperwork and unmade decisions will fall on those we love. Hunting for a will or an insurance policy or a password is a trying task while we grieve. An aging couple I know updates this information each Valentine's Day as a love gift to one another.

I suspect the habit of denying that we will die is rooted in a tremendously confusing dichotomy. We identify with our physical bodies and lives. I am a human being, I say. You are a man or a woman. I am a writer, a teacher, a mother. You are tall or short, old or young. How often do we describe ourselves as spirit or soul, as that aspect that does not die? Yet part of us is always aware of our deathless aspect. We perch uncomfortably on the twin prongs of our fear that we will die and our conviction that we won't. Why make a contact plan or write a will when there will always be tomorrow? Death and all that surrounds it are a huge challenge, yet it won't jinx our lives to face our deaths. It won't bring death on. Perhaps we can even discover that death is not the enemy we had perceived it to be.

౼

Finding the courage to face the future reality of our own deaths can also allow us to be more present when someone we know experiences a loss. Long ago I met a woman whose name I don't recall, wearing a T-shirt that read, "Ask me about Al." I asked her about Al. Al was her teenaged son who had died in a motorcycle accident. She had the shirt printed because with the best of intentions acquaintances and even friends shunned the bombed-out wreckage this left within her as if their silence would make her grief disappear. I experienced similar evasions after Randi's death. Not having learned what to say, often people either avoided me entirely or avoided my eyes and chatted about the weather. Those able to address me directly gave me the gift of their compassionate presence in simple ways: "How are you *doing*?" asked with an expression and a tone that indicated they genuinely wanted to know, while their body language said they had all the time in the world. Or the friend who'd never met Randi who asked to see photos of her. It wasn't that I wanted to review the details of her depression or her death; what I longed to do was to talk about her life. A question like, "What kind of a child was she?' was like being offered a glass of champagne. As friends who could be present with me watched me come back to being myself again, I suspect we all benefited by becoming a little more at ease with the whole area of death and of grief.

ℰℑ

Reading one or a few of the books on death and dying and after-death communication in my bibliography can assist us to become more comfortable with death and to familiarize us with even more of ADC's possibilities. So can going outside and allowing nature to speak to us. A silent walk through the woods may be a time to look and listen for contact with a dead beloved. Nature is a wise teacher. If we pay close attention, we will notice the constant presence and intermingling of death and new life. Nature is a gentle place to experiment too, to ask that a bird or a butterfly link us to our dead, or just to ask for a sign that they are with us. Awareness may or may not come. We may be given the opportunity to choose between gratitude and doubt, or between exercising patience and shouting out, "Where the hell are you?"

ℰℑ

Consider the classic methods we use to communicate— talking, writing, the visual arts, ceremony—consider our own preferences. Would we rather talk over tea or write a note? Am I more receptive when doing something physical like walking or bicycling? Do you like creating something with your hands? If I pray, is it easier in a house of worship, under a tree, or in my own home? When indigenous people use ceremony to contact the dead, this can be elaborate, but the essence of ceremony is simple. Think of Isabel in chapter 1 who lit two candles when her electricity went off and asked, "If my father were to visit me, I wonder how he would let me know he was here?" He snuffed out one candle in answer. Focus and intention, two candles—they needed nothing more to connect.

I spoke once at a grief therapy class in which artist Aline Fourier had the group create doorways to invite our dead to make contact. She supplied a cabinet chock-full of paper, glue, fabric, ribbons, feathers, tempera paint, and more. I loved the doing of this. The layered and complex arched doorway I made still hangs on my wall, but I did not receive contact in this way, though others did. A woodworker or metalworker or sculptor might create a more three-dimensional version of this doorway.

❧

Words are a more effective tool for me, though not for everyone. If we keep a journal, if writing helps us figure out our lives, writing letters to and from the dead may be in harmony with us. I suggest combining the process with some ceremony: a candle, a spritz of rose water, carefully selected pen and paper, a quiet and uninterrupted time. Address and date the letter as if the person were still alive and let the words pour out on the page without censorship. Be real. Express your anger, jealousy, loneliness, your grief. Save the letter or burn or bury it. Mail it to a fictitious address or to yourself. Write again and again if desired. This may be enough, or there is an additional possibility that can lead to transformative healing, especially in troubled or difficult relationships. That is, to reverse roles and write a response back from the person to whom we have written. Each time I have taught and led this exercise, there has been at least one person who achieved a breakthrough of understanding. Be forewarned though, such a letter can be exceedingly difficult to start. Don't be afraid to begin with something like, "If I knew what you would want to say, I would write . . ." Imagination is the key, allowing the words to arise with as little doubt as possible until they come as though the person were dictating them. If this doesn't happen, abandon this method and try another, or write a second, third, or fourth letter until it does.

એ

To die from the body is to merge with the world of Spirit. We embodied ones are a part of that world as well, but we tend to be so distracted by the material realm, we are often barely aware of this. Our minds overflow with activity like airport terminals the day before Thanksgiving. What can we do to slow this activity down and to still our restless bodies, to step into a listening and observing posture that makes a space through which communication from our dead beloveds can be more readily received? By consistently attempting to become consciously aware of our connection with the Divine, we align ourselves with the unseen, acknowledge its presence, and set the stage for participating in an exchange with it.

Any spiritual practice trains us to move beyond our five senses. I don't see that there are right and wrong ways to go about this. Temple, church, mosque, prayer, meditation, contemplation, silence, mantras, singing, chanting, making art, meditative dance all have potential to strengthen our connection to the God-force. Our relationship with the Divine is personal. Prayer and meditation are one-on-one activities, though they may be done within a group and many of us find a community of like-minded people supports the process. The main factor is to look for what resonates, begin, and stay with it.

Decades ago I began my commitment to a spirit-practice with a mere two minutes daily. I was busy all the time. I had a job, a husband, two children at home, pets, a garden. An every-day-without-fail meditation practice eluded me for months. I'd manage twenty minutes on Monday, then miss Tuesday and Wednesday. Consistent discipline seemed impossible until the day I realized I could be two minutes late for nearly everything in my life without serious repercussion. I remember meditating for those two minutes perched on the edge of the couch with my coat on, car keys in hand, because I'd almost headed out the door for work before I remembered. Now, only serious bleeding would cause me to forget. I'd sooner leave the house with scummy teeth than without doing my spirit-practice, though its length has extended well beyond those original two minutes.

You have read how my mantra practice draws my daughter's presence. Sibyl's experience has been similar. Her life is so profoundly centered on the spiritual, she says she often feels a deepening of intimacy with someone after death, that the connecting points may be more robust with the dead than with a living person whose life focus is more secular. She is often aware of her mother and sister (though she adds that her father sometimes "piggybacks" on their presence) as she is engaged in her spiritual practice of chanting in Aramaic, the Semitic language ancestral to Hebrew.

℘

The paradox of all these methods, techniques, and tools is that eventually we need to remember to breathe and stop trying to make anything happen. We need to learn to allow the deaths of our beloveds to be what they are and to breathe and figure out how to continue living. If we can permit ourselves to trust that they are with us, whether or not we see or hear or feel their presence with our physical senses, peace can eventually bathe us in its transcendent light. It is confirming and wonderful and vibrant and relieving and a great comfort to experience the more phenomenal versions of after-death contact, but we need not feel deprived without these, for our dead beloveds are with us.

Most of what surrounds death in modern times is an attempt to make death go away. Once, we died at home. Our children and grandchildren played on the floor beside our deathbeds. Our bodies were washed by our daughters and sisters. Our coffins were built by our sons and brothers. Wakes were held in our parlors. Now many of us die in hospitals. Even when we are seriously ill and death is expected and imminent, when it actually starts to darken our sickroom doors, the ambulance may be called. Then, instead of seeing the faces and hearing the voices and feeling the touch of our beloveds, it is sirens and strangers and medical equipment that witness and accompany our last breaths. Coffins may be lined with steel to preserve the illusion that decay will not occur. We wear no mourning. We are urged to return to our jobs quickly. At work, a new widow's apology for a moment of distracted sorrow four months after the fact elicits a puzzled expression and the question, "You're not over that yet?"

We may not expect contact after death. If we receive it, we may be afraid to tell anyone. If we do, we may be called deluded. You have read of the variety of ADC experiences and their lack of limitations. You have read that the veil, though opaque in certain lights, is often penetrated. If we look through closed eyelids, if we filter our gaze and sidestep the pitfalls of our mental machinations, it is feasible, even likely, that we can sense the presence of our dead beloveds. You have seen that one of death's innumerable teachings is to urge us to look in a new way, to experience with a different sense, to explore the unseen worlds. You have seen that we cannot count the ways in which contact may come, because what I have shown here is only what I have shown here. Were I to continue on, or you to take over for me, and interview a hundred more and a hundred more, to write another and yet another book, the types and ways of contact would continue to surprise.

This project will not find an end. Months ago I arbitrarily ceased the formal interview process in order to get on with completing the book, yet this week alone, when I stopped by a friend's house, unbidden she shared an ADC dream of dancing with her grandmother, the feel of her skin as real and as warm as in life. In a thrift shop, as I helped my newly pregnant granddaughter Chelsey choose baby clothes, I met another friend who had just been told by a young woman that she knows her dead friend is okay, because he has come and told her so. My AARP magazine arrived in the mail. Flipping through it as I waited for tea water to heat, I browsed an article about cruises, though I'm not interested in cruises. The widowed author ends by sharing the first dream of her husband since his death. She describes it as "amazingly realistic, the way such dreams usually are."[3] She told him she'd been to Venice, where he had once lived; he seemed already aware of her trip. This is clearly an ADC dream and in a mainstream magazine. My granddaughter reported seeing five hawks on the way to visit us for Mother's Day and seven on the drive home, a blessing from her mother on her new pregnancy.

We are as surrounded by examples of after-death communication as we are by the denial of it. Does a mention in the AARP magazine mean acceptance may soon win out over denial, or is this just my personal desire? All I can be certain of is that we can expect and look for after-death communication, though we cannot predict whether it will come or how or when.

Because there are so many who have experienced contact, it is easy to believe this is a universal experience, and there is the possibility that it is. To be aware of contact is something else again. Grief may cloud our vision. The loneliness of him or her not coming home for dinner may make us ungrateful for a visit in a dream. An eagle flies by the window after a woman's husband's death; it stays in the yard all day as people come and go—not your usual eagle behavior. Months later, in bed, she pleads with her beloved to hold her hand one time more. He does not. The next morning as she drives to work, she sees a pair of eagles clutching their talons together as they plummet through the sky. This is a part of their mating ritual, but she does not want mating eagles. She wants her beloved to hold *her* hand.

No matter how much connection we have, the death state is not the same as the living state, and we are only too aware of that. The other side of the veil—no matter how porous or sheer that veil may be—is still not the physical realm. A single touch is a comfort, but it is not the same as the frequent embraces of daily physical life. Though my contact with my daughter has been a gift so far beyond measure I can barely touch it with words, she is also absent from my life in the way she was once present. To say that I don't miss her would be an exercise in denial.

Existence is vast and luscious and expansive, and it is our role as humans to explore its outer reaches, not to confine and limit them. What I want to convey is the rich mystery of the interpenetration of the various levels of this reality. Existence is not an either/or affair. It is not that if I am happy, I can't be sad; if I am here, I can't be there; if I don't see it, it doesn't exist; if my beloved dies, he or she is gone. Part of our task is to come into relationship with this interpenetration, to trust the unseen and the subtle. Often this is called faith—or when spoken of in a derogatory way, even blind faith—but there is another path that is about allowing ourselves to see and to know in these realms where neither blindness nor faith is involved. Religions often have two arms: one based on faith or a firm belief in something that cannot be proven and the other, the mystical arm, steeped in direct experience of the transcendent or communion with the God-force. This allows the light of inner knowing and deep conviction to awaken within us. This experiential path—though still not provable to another—is where after-death contact lives. Because we are all touched by death, because anyone who loves has the potential to receive communication through the veil between the living and the dead, we all share the possibility of experiencing the mystical, to become, to one extent or another, if for only a single moment, a mystic.

As we leave behind our bodies and slip through the diaphanous veil, we will experience its permeability. It looks like many of us quickly determine that if it can be penetrated one way, it can be penetrated the other way, so we return and visit the living. Most of us don't spend our days and nights on the meditation pillow or on our knees. We don't spend long hours spinning like Sufi dancers. We are not wandering sadhus who beg for food and seek divine wisdom in every moment of every day. We are showing up on the job, paying the rent or mortgage, diapering the baby, checking our cell phones, cooking spaghetti. The mystical may elude us, but death will not. It will touch us all and touch us more than once. If we love, when death comes to our beloveds, it will be painful for us. It will also offer us the promise of deep and life-altering mystical moments. Death and what follows—communication through the veil—may be the ordinary person's most transparent entrée into mystical experience. The stories I have shared here are neither science fiction nor fairy tale. We need not close this book and blink our way out into the light, as we do from a movie matinee, emerging back into the real world. After-death communication *is* of the real world. It is magnificent. And it is within reach.

– THE END –

Notes

Preface

1. The Institute of Noetic Sciences *(noetic.org)* is an organization that encourages exploration of consciousness at the nexus of science and spirit.

2. Oliver Sacks, *Hallucinations* (New York: Alfred A. Knopf, 2012), p. 236.

3. From Russell's essay, "What Is an Agnostic?" in *The Basic Writings of Bertrand Russell*, edited by Robert E. Egner and Lester E. Dennonn (New York: Simon & Schuster, 1961), p. 583.

4. Isaac Bashevis Singer, "Inventions," *The New Yorker* (January 26, 2015): 67–69. This story was written in 1965 but not published in English until 2015.

Introduction

1. Michael Ortiz Hill and Mandaza Augustine Kandemwa, *Twin from Another Tribe: The Story of Two Shamanic Healers from Africa and North America* (Wheaton, IL: Quest Books, 2007), p. 32.

2. Edward Hirsch, *How to Read a Poem: And Fall in Love with Poetry* (San Diego: Harcourt, 1999), p. xi.

CHAPTER ONE

1. Stan Tekiela, *Birds of New Mexico: Field Guide* (Cambridge, MN: Adventure Publications, 2004), p. 281.

2. Vine Deloria Jr., *God Is Red: A Native View of Religion* (Golden, CO: Fulcrum Publishing, 2003), p. 295.

CHAPTER TWO

1. Patricia Garfield, *The Dream Messenger: How Dreams of the Departed Bring Healing Gifts* (New York: Simon & Schuster, 1997), pp. 86–88.

2. Michael Newton, *Destiny of Souls: New Case Studies of Life Between Lives* (St. Paul, MN: Llewellyn Publications, 2000), p. 154.

3. The hypnagogic state lies just before, and the hypnopompic state comes right after, a period of sleep. These times can be places of semiconscious dreaming or visions.

CHAPTER THREE

1. Helen Greaves, *Testimony of Light* (London, England: Rider, an imprint of Ebury Press, Random House, 2004), p. 65.

CHAPTER FOUR

1. Ohky Simine Forest, *Dreaming the Council Ways: True Native Teachings from the Red Lodge* (York Beach, Maine: Red Wheel/ Samuel Weiser, 2000), p. 34.

CHAPTER FIVE

1. Vine Deloria Jr., *God is Red: A Native View of Religion* (Golden, CO: Fulcrum Publishing, 2003), p. 170.

2. Dorothy Bryant, *The Kin of Ata Are Waiting for You* (New York and Berkeley, CA, Random House and Moon Books, 1983).

CHAPTER SEVEN

1. My interviewee, Rita, pointed out that the left is our receptive side. As you know, except when my daughter floods my entire

body with her presence, she usually visits on my left. Asked why, she replied she was showing my left brain (the logical, doubting-Thomas side) that our contact was real. My mother, however, who sometimes accompanies my daughter, invariably visits on my right. It seems to me this is just another idiosyncratic manner in which the dead make their own choices in visiting us.

CHAPTER EIGHT

1. Reiki is a Japanese technique to reduce stress, promote relaxation, and encourage healing.

2. Galway Kinnell, *A New Selected Poems* (Boston and New York, Houghton Mifflin Company, 2000), p. 116.

CHAPTER TEN

1. Yvette Melanson with Claire Safran, *Looking for Lost Bird: A Jewish Woman Discovers her Navajo Roots* (New York: Perennial/Harper/Collins, 1999), pp. 50–51.

2. The Five Wishes document—available online—is a living will, written in everyday language, to initiate conversations and clarify issues concerning care in serious illness. It is designed to let both loved ones and doctors know our wishes about medical care and the end of our lives. It is a legal document in most of the United States. *www.agingwithdignity.org/five-wishes*.

3. Myrna Blythe, "A Sentimental Journey: A Trip for One Brings up Old Memories and Yields New Discoveries," *AARP, The Magazine* (April/May 2015): 29–31 and 80.

Selected Bibliography

This bibliography is not intended to be a comprehensive listing of all resources relevant to after-death communication. Instead it is an idiosyncratic selection that includes books I've come across quite by accident, books I've loved, read, and reread, and even a few I've found disappointing, though so applicable I've included them anyway. I have annotated most items to help you select among them.

After-death Communication

Arcangel, Dianne. *Afterlife Encounters: Ordinary People, Extraordinary Experiences.* Charlottesville, VA: Hampton Roads Publishing, 2005. Arcangel, former director of the Elisabeth Kübler-Ross Center of Houston, based her book on the experiences of her hospice patients and on the results of her online Afterlife Encounter Survey.

Barker, Elsa. *Letters from the Light: An Afterlife Journal from the Self-Lighted World.* Hillsboro, OR: Beyond Words Publishing, 1995, originally published in 1914. The author's friend, Judge Hatch, dictated this book to her after his death. He relates many details about his particular experience in the afterlife.

Devers, Edie, PhD. *Goodbye Again: Experiences with Departed Loved Ones.* Kansas City: Andrews and McMeel, 1997. Inspired by the positive changes Devers saw in her sister after an ADC with their mother, the author went on to research this field, earn her PhD, and become a psychotherapist.

Greaves, Helen. *Testimony of Light*. London, England: Rider, an imprint of Ebury Press, Random House, 2004, originally published in 1969. The author's friend, who had spent twenty-five years as an Anglican sister before leaving the church to explore other spiritual approaches, communicated the text of this book after her death.

Guggenheim, Bill and Judy. *Hello from Heaven! A New Field of Research—After-Death Communication—Confirms That Life and Love Are Eternal*. New York: Bantam Books, 1996 (paperback edition, 1997). A thorough, 353-page compendium of the results of seven years collecting ADC accounts from 2,000 people for The ADC Project they founded in 1988. It was the Guggenheims who coined the phrase after-death communication and its acronym ADC.

LaGrand, Louis E., PhD. *After Death Communication: Final Farewells*. St. Paul, MN: Llewellyn Publications, 1997; and *Messages and Miracles: Extraordinary Experiences of the Bereaved*. St. Paul, MN: Llewellyn Publications, 1999; and *Loves Lives On: Learning from the Extraordinary Encounters of the Bereaved*. New York: Berkley Books, 2006. Grief therapist LaGrand shares many of his clients' ADC experiences within the context of healing grief, which he sees as the purpose of contact. Like the Guggenheims in *Hello from Heaven!*, he is excited by "evidential" experiences that "prove" ADC is real. *Love Lives On* is primarily a self-help book for those in grief.

Moody, Raymond, MD, with Paul Perry. *Reunions: Visionary Encounters with Departed Loved Ones*. New York: Villard Books, a division of Random House; Toronto; and Random House of Canada, 1993. Moody, author of the 1975 book *Life after Life*, describes a technique he has developed called "mirror gazing" for initiating contact with dead beloveds.

Morse, Melvin, MD, with Paul Perry. *Parting Visions: Uses and Meanings of Pre-Death, Psychic, and Spiritual Experiences*. New

York: Villard Books, a division of Random House, 1994. Morse, a pediatrician, covers what he calls "death-related visions" that help both children and adults with grief and with dying. He has written other books about children's near-death experiences.

DREAMS

Bosnak, Robert. *A Little Course on Dreams: A Basic Handbook of Jungian Dreamwork*. Boston: Shambhala Publications, Inc., 1988. This tiny book is a gem, a favorite of mine, and as useful to a reader just getting into dreamwork as to one already engaged by it. He suggests exercises for dream recall, dream reentry, and dream amplification.

Garfield, Patricia. *The Dream Messenger: How Dreams of the Departed Bring Healing Gifts*. New York: Simon & Schuster, 1997. Founder of the Association for the Study of Dreams, Garfield gives a thorough overview, with examples, of the many types of ADC dreams. Her earlier book, *Creative Dreaming* (1974), is a mainstay in dream literature. I read it years ago and still use certain of her techniques on a daily basis.

Moss, Robert. *The Dreamer's Book of the Dead: A Soul Traveler's Guide to Death, Dying, and The Other Side*. Rochester, NY: Destiny Books, 2005. The book expands well beyond its title to cover more general information on dreaming.

Taylor, Jeremy. *Where People Fly and Water Runs Uphill: Using Dreams to Tap the Wisdom of the Unconscious*. New York: Warner Books, 1992. A wise and practical book in which Taylor not only addresses how we benefit from our individual dreams but gives guidelines for setting up a dream group and exploring dreams in a group setting. This is only one of his several books on dreams.

Waggoner, Robert. *Lucid Dreaming: Gateway to the Inner Self*. Needham, MA: Moment Point Press, 2009. Waggoner's broad-ranging approach includes his personal lifelong exploration of lucid dreaming. He ends with tips for everyone from those who hope to lucid dream through those who are already experienced lucid dreamers.

GRIEF, DEATH AND DYING,
AND END-OF-LIFE ISSUES

Bartlow, Bruce G., MD. *Medical Care of the Soul: A Practical and Healing Guide to End-of-Life Issues for Families, Patients, and Healthcare Providers*. Boulder, CO: Johnson Books, 2000. The title says it well. Bartlow brings compassion, hope, and wisdom to his topic. He doesn't shy away from the spiritual aspects of death either.

Budge, E. A. Wallis (introduction and English translation). *The Book of the Dead: The Hieroglyphic of the Transcript of the Papyrus of ANI*. Secaucus, NJ: University Books, Inc., 1960. A dense, 704-page collection of funerary texts named *The Book of the Dead* by the pioneer nineteenth-century Egyptologists. However, because it is put together in sections and well-indexed, dipping in and out of it is easy to do.

Cope, Denys, RN, BSN. *Dying: A Natural Passage*. Santa Fe, NM: Three Whale Publishing, LLC, 2008. During the many years Cope spent working with the dying, she photocopied a packet of information as a tool to assist families to better understand the changes occurring as their loved ones were dying. That packet was the seed for this little book, designed to be quickly read as our beloveds lie dying.

Didion, Joan. *The Year of Magical Thinking*. New York: Alfred A. Knopf, 2005. Didion richly captures the reality of the year following her husband's death, demonstrating her painfully slow rise through and out of deep grief.

Edelman, Hope. *Motherless Daughters: The Legacy of Loss*. Reading, MA: Addison-Wesley Publishing Company, 1994. This collection of stories (including her own) about the often lengthy or recurrent grief process of women whose mothers die when their daughters are young was a useful tool for understanding my granddaughter's grief process. She wasn't ready to read the book herself, but when I copied a few key pages, she read those and taped them into her journal.

Gawande, Atul. *Being Mortal: Medicine and What Matters in the End*. New York: Metropolitan Books, Henry Holt and Company, 2014. Like Bruce Bartlow, Gawande is a medical doctor who sees a need to renovate how both patients and doctors relate to death. When he addresses how his father's aging, lengthy illness, and death changed the way he attends to his own patients, his intimate stance is moving.

Heart, Rosalie Deer. *Healing Grief: A Mother's Story*. San Cristobal, NM: Heart Link Publications, 1996. Includes both the author's own after-death contact with her son and that of her two-and-a-half-year-old daughter with her brother.

Jordan, Wendy. *Embracing the End-of-Life Journey*. Bloomington, IN: Balboa Press, a division of Hay House, 2014. Jordan writes from the caring perspective of a Reiki practitioner who gives treatments to both the dying and their family members.

Kübler-Ross, Elisabeth, MD. *On Death and Dying*. New York: Collier Books, Macmillan Publishing Company, 1969. The classic book on amending our view of death and how we cope with it, where she introduces her five stages of grief and dying. Her numerous other books include *On Children and Death* (1983) and *On Life after Death* (1991).

Levine, Stephen. *Who Dies? An Investigation of Conscious Living and Conscious Dying* (1982); *Meetings at the Edge* (1984); *Healing into Life and Death* (1987); and *A Gradual Awakening* (1989), all published in New York by Anchor Books, Doubleday. Levine's books were part of my earliest readings on death as I became a hospice volunteer. They offer a profound, simple, insightful—even tender—approach to dying and death, and include various healing meditation techniques.

Morris, Virginia. *Talking about Death Won't Kill You*. New York: Workman Publishing, 2001. The title reveals the book—readable, personal, pragmatic, down-to-earth.

Nuland, Sherwin B., MD. *How We Die: Reflections on Life's Final Chapter*. New York: Alfred A. Knopf, 1994. This was a Pulitzer Prize finalist. Nuland, a surgeon, has been involved in the dying process of many patients. His death descriptions can be quite clinical, yet he manages to soften this information with his sensitive approach.

Redfern, Suzanne, and Susan K. Gilbert. *The Grieving Garden: Living with the Death of a Child.* Charlottesville, VA: Hampton Roads Publishing, 2008. Twenty-two parents tell the story of dealing with the deaths of their children.

Sogyal Rinpoche. *The Tibetan Book of Living and Dying.* San Francisco: Harper San Francisco, 1992. Although Sogyal Rinpoche focuses on Tibetan Buddhist beliefs and practices, he illuminates death beyond this scope. The book is relevant and accessible for non-Buddhist readers interested in deepening their grasp of both death and life.

Starr, Mirabai. *Caravan of No Despair: A Memoir of Loss and Transformation.* Louisville, CO: Sounds True, 2015. Starr's memoir ranges from her childhood in the sixties on into the present, but her statement that "My spiritual life began with the death of my daughter" is at the heart of the book.

Worth, Jennifer. *In the Midst of Life.* London, England: Phoenix, an imprint of Orion Books Ltd., 2011. A British nurse, Worth says that just like birth, death is not dignified and that dying in peace may be a better goal than dying with dignity.

NEAR-DEATH EXPERIENCES

Alexander, Eben, MD. *Proof of Heaven: A Neurosurgeon's Journey into the Afterlife.* New York: Simon & Schuster Paperbacks, 2012. Alexander's NDE while his body lay in a coma transformed his entire life and belief system. Now he devotes much of his time to the exploration of spiritually transformative experiences and other consciousness-related issues through his organization Eternea *(www.Eternea.org)*.

Moorjani, Anita. *Dying to Be Me: My Journey from Cancer, to Near Death, to True Healing.* Carlsbad, CA: Hay House, Inc., 2012. Moorjani received information in her NDE that showed her the cause of her cancer and led to her healing.

Ring, Kenneth. *Heading toward Omega: In Search of the Meaning of the Near-death Experience*. New York: Quill, William Morrow, 1985; and (with Evelyn Elsaesser Valarino) *Lessons from the Light: What We Can Learn from the Near-death Experience*. Needham, MA: Moment Point Press, 2006. Ring is an early NDE researcher who tells fascinating stories in both books. In the second he also makes a case for studying NDEs as a way to bring some of their lessons into our own lives.

OTHER RELATED BOOKS AND WORKS CITED

Assante, Julia, PhD. *The Last Frontier: Exploring the Afterlife and Transforming Our Fear of Death*. Novato, CA: New World Library, 2012. Both a scholar and a psychic, Assante takes a broad, historical look at the afterlife, covering everything from quantum physics to her first personal after-death communication with a beloved.

Athie, Francisco. *Vera*. Mexico/USA/France/Germany, 2003, available in the United States through *facets.org*. This stunning and magical film depicts an old Maya man as he journeys from life into death with Vera as his guide. It is in Mayan and Spanish with English subtitles, but there is so little need for language the subtitles seem almost irrelevant.

Blythe, Myrna. "A Sentimental Journey: A Trip for One Brings up Old Memories and Yields New Discoveries." *AARP, The Magazine* (April/May 2015): 29–31 and 80.

Deloria, Vine Jr. *God Is Red: A Native View of Religion*. Golden, CO: Fulcrum Publishing, 1992. First published in 1972, this definitive book, written by a Native American theologian, historian, and activist, is still in print in 2015 with good reason. It offers a rich opportunity to see life (and death) from a Native American perspective.

Egner, Robert E., and Lester E. Dennonn, eds. *The Basic Writings of Bertrand Russell*. New York: Simon & Schuster, 1961.

Forest, Ohky Simine. *Dreaming the Council Ways: True Native Teachings from the Red Lodge*. York Beach, Maine: Samuel

Weiser, 2000. Another indigenous take on life and death, this time from a Canadian of Mohawk and French parents who is an initiated Maya shaman in Chiapas, Mexico. She now spells her first name Ohki.

Heath, Pamela Rae, and Jon Klimo. *Suicide: What Really Happens in the Afterlife: Channeled Conversations with the Dead.* Berkeley, CA: North Atlantic Books, 2006. Heath is a parapsychology expert. Klimo is an authority on channeling.

Hill, Michael Ortiz, and Mandaza Augustine Kandemwa. *Twin from Another Planet: The Story of Two Shamanic Healers from Africa and North America.* Wheaton, IL: Quest Books, 2007. In alternating chapters these two healers discuss their service to spirit on two continents.

Hirsch, Edward. *How to Read a Poem: And Fall in Love with Poetry.* San Diego: Harcourt, 1999.

Ingerman, Sandra. *Shamanic Journeying: A Beginner's Guide.* Boulder, CO: Sounds True, 2004 (includes drumming CD). I have studied and journeyed with Ingerman, who is a consummate teacher. Her book is a way to enter the art of journeying in order to go beyond ordinary reality and claim information to enhance our lives.

Melanson, Yvette, with Claire Safran. *Looking for Lost Bird: A Jewish Woman Discovers Her Navajo Roots.* New York: Perennial/Harper/Collins, 1999. Relates the author's ADC with her adoptive mother that I refer to in chapter 10.

Newton, Michael. *Journey of Souls: Case Studies of Life between Lives* (1996); *Destiny of Souls: New Case Studies of Life Between Lives* (2002); and *Memories of the Afterlife: Life between Lives: Stories of Personal Transformation* (2011), all published in St. Paul, MN by Llewellyn Publications. This hypnotherapist sheds light on the afterlife by relating what his clients have said during sessions about their experiences before this life and between their other lives. These people have much to say regarding soul agreements. I especially recommend the first two books.

Sacks, Oliver. *Hallucinations*. New York: Alfred A. Knopf, 2012. This is a book on hallucinations as symptoms of mental illness. The relevance to my subject is contrarian, because Sacks devotes part of chapter 13, "The Haunted Mind" (pp. 229–54) to debunking after-death communication. I feel particularly disappointed by this, since I have been a Sacks fan for years, ever since reading his early book *The Man Who Mistook His Wife for a Hat*.

Sherwood, Christine. *Fire & Ash: The Alchemy of Cancer*. Taos, NM: Nighthawk Press, 2014. Though this is prose, its lyrical language reveals the author's roots as a poet. Her memoir relates to my situation in that we each received our experience as an opportunity to connect with Spirit and to search for meaning within our suffering.

Singer, Isaac Bashevis. "Inventions." *The New Yorker* (January 26, 2015): 67–69. This story was written in 1965 but not published in English until 2015.

ABOUT THE AUTHOR

Photo by Michael Walsh

The After Death Chronicles is Annie Mattingley's first book, unless, she says, you count the "practice books" that she burned or buried or never wrote beyond fifty pages. The large questions of existence, especially those that lie on the cusp between life and death, have been central to her life, leading her to earn her MA in Interdisciplinary Consciousness Studies.

She has co-published an engineering magazine, taught Journal-Writing as a Healing Art in universities, worked for a film festival, volunteered with hospice, and has long been guided by her dreams. Following a similar serpentine path, she has lived in five states from coast to coast and has now settled in the sixth, New Mexico, with her husband, in the morning shadow of the Sangre de Cristo Mountains with a hundred-mile view from her front door. She has two daughters (one living and one deceased), one stepson, two grandchildren, and one very new great-granddaughter. She is now retired and lives in Questa, New Mexico. Visit her at *www.anniemattingley.com*.